Easy Cake Decorating COOKBOOK

by Mildred Brand

Ideals Publishing Corp.
Milwaukee, Wisconsin

Introduction

When I was twelve years old, my grandmother gave me a decorating set consisting of a metal cylinder and several changeable ends. I was intrigued with it and used it to decorate all kinds of food. A few years later I was fascinated to watch a demonstrator use a metal tube and a bag to make beautiful roses with icing. I had to have a set immediately.

Through my early married years I practiced on my seven children's birthday cakes and on cakes to give to friends on special occasions.

In 1960, I finally took my first professional cake decorating class in Chicago and after that session I was really hooked! Since then I have taken many classes in various methods of decorating from instructors throughout the United States.

Easy Cake Decorating contains step-by-step instructions in the basics of cake decorating, including flowers, borders and special techniques which can be used both by beginning and experienced cake decorators. And the book is arranged so that it can be used as a textbook as well as allowing homemakers to teach themselves.

Cake decorating is fun! And beautifully decorated cakes are a delight to share with family and friends. So start practicing the art today and create cakes you will be proud to give.

Contents

ISBN 0-89542-622-6

Copyright © by Mildred Brand 1980
Milwaukee, Wisconsin 53201
All rights reserved.
Printed and bound in the U.S.A.
Published simultaneously in Canada.
Published by Ideals Publishing Corporation
11315 Watertown Plank Road
Milwaukee, Wisconsin 53226

Equipment

Decorating Bags

There are two basic types of decorating bags, plastic-coated and parchment. The plastic-coated bags are pliable, reusable and dishwasher safe. The other type of bag is the parchment cone, which is purchased as a flat, triangular sheet of paper and then rolled into a cone.

How to make a parchment cone

1. Hold the triangle pointed side down and wide side up.
2. Grasp the left side of the triangle with the left hand and use the right hand to form a cone. Bringing the right upper point down toward the tip, align the point formed at the top with the bottom tip.
3. With the left hand, wrap the left side of the triangle around the cone, pulling the points close together. Adjust the points until the tip is very tight.
4. Place the cone on the table. Press sharp creases in the cone to hold its shape. Fold the points in. The seams of the cone must overlap completely to the point so that the bag will not tear when pressure is applied.
5. The bag may be taped to keep it more securely closed. Do *not* staple the bag.
6. Trim approximately ½ inch from the top of the cone.
7. Drop the tube through the center of the bag so that it falls through the opening.

Closing the Bag

1. Fill the bag no more than half full of icing.
2. Fold each corner in; then fold the top down.
3. Twist twice just below the top.

Later, if using a large quantity of icing in a single color, you may use a large decorating bag which holds more icing. Fasten the top with a rubber band. Push the excess icing toward the rubber band and then twist the bag so that it fits snugly into your hand. As additional icing is needed, work a small portion at a time down from the top, twisting the area where the bag is held, to keep the excess separated from the icing being used.

Couplers

Couplers are an invaluable aid in cake decorating. They are used with the decorating bag to allow a change of tubes without emptying the bag. This is especially important when several tubes will be used with the same color of icing.

Couplers may be used with either type of decorating bag, although they work best with the plastic-coated permanent type bag.

How to use a coupler

1. Remove the ring from the main part of the coupler.
2. Trim the decorating bag, a small amount at a time, so that when the coupler is inserted into the tip of the bag, at least two threads will be exposed.
3. Push the coupler down into the decorating bag.
4. Place a tube over the end of the coupler. Secure it by screwing the ring over the tube and onto the main part of the coupler.

Food Colors

Food color is available at cake decorating supply outlets. The best types are paste and liquid paste, which can be combined to create lovely pastels as well as rich, deep shades of color.

Deep colors require large amounts of paste, but black and dark brown can be achieved by adding paste to chocolate icing.

Below is a chart of custom colors that can be made by combining the colors listed.

How to mix food color

When mixing food color with icing, separate a small portion of icing and blend thoroughly with color; then combine it with the remaining icing. When more than one food color is used, blend one color at a time with a small portion of the icing and then combine with the remaining icing.

Custom Colors

Aqua Leaf Green + Slight Royal Blue	**Coral** Red-Red + Yellow	**Poppy** Red + Orange
Avocado Leaf Green + Orange or Brown	**Cranberry** Royal Red + Slight Brown + Slight Lavender	**Ruby Red** Royal Red + Yellow
Bronze Brown + Yellow + Red	**Flesh** White + Copper Brown	**Rust** Copper Brown or Brown + Slight Red + Slight Yellow
Burgundy Dark Red + Slight Lavender + Slight Blue	**Ivory** White + Slight Brown + Slight Yellow or White + Egg Yellow	**Steel Blue** Royal Blue + Slight Black
Chartreuse Leaf Green + Slight Lemon Yellow	**Plum** Violet + Red	**Turquoise** Sky Blue + Slight Green

Decorating Icings

Buttercream Icing

Use this icing for practice. It's easy to make as well as great tasting. Makes good borders. Excellent icing for any cake.

   5 tablespoons water
   ½ cup vegetable shortening, or high ratio shortening*
   1 teaspoon vanilla
   ¼ teaspoon butter flavoring
   ½ teaspoon almond flavoring
   ½ teaspoon salt
   1 pound confectioners' sugar, sifted

Combine all ingredients and beat on high speed until well blended, about ten minutes. Blend five additional minutes on low speed.

Royal Icing

This icing can also be made by using Picture Icing Mix, which is sold commercially.

   ⅔ cup water
   4 tablespoons meringue powder
   ½ teaspoon cream of tartar
   2 pounds confectioners' sugar, sifted
   1 tablespoon gum arabic

Combine water, meringue powder and cream of tartar in a small mixing bowl and beat until stiff peaks form. Combine confectioners' sugar and gum arabic and mix thoroughly. Add to meringue. Beat on low speed until stiff peaks are formed.

Flower Decorator Icing

This icing makes sharp, well-defined flowers and is best suited for this. It does not make a good frosting.

   1 cup plus 2 tablespoons vegetable shortening or high ratio shortening*
   1 egg white
   ½ teaspoon salt
   1 pound confectioners' sugar, sifted
   ½ teaspoon vanilla

Combine shortening, egg white, salt and vanilla. Gradually add half of the confectioners' sugar. Continue mixing at lowest speed of mixer until well blended. Add remaining sugar and mix slowly until free of lumps.

Boiled Icing with Meringue Powder

Very good for border work on wedding cakes and figure piping on novelty cakes. Icing can be stored and rebeaten as needed.

   ½ cup meringue powder
   1 cup water
   1 pound confectioners' sugar, sifted
   ¼ cup water
   1 cup granulated sugar
   ¼ teaspoon cream of tartar

Beat meringue powder and one cup water together in a stationary mixer at high speed until soft peaks form. Add confectioners' sugar and continue to beat until smooth. Meanwhile, combine the one-quarter cup water, granulated sugar and cream of tartar in a small saucepan. Cover tightly and bring to a boil. Continue to boil until syrup boils freely and steam comes from under the lid. Remove lid and insert a candy thermometer. Boil until temperature reaches 250°. Pour hot syrup over meringue and beat constantly until smooth.

Boiled Icing with Egg Whites

This icing is easy to work with but does not rebeat well.

   2 cups granulated sugar
   ½ cup water
   ½ teaspoon cream of tartar
   4 egg whites
   1½ cups confectioners' sugar, sifted

Combine sugar, water and cream of tartar in a small saucepan; cover. When steam rises freely from under the lid, insert thermometer and boil to 250°. Meanwhile, beat the egg whites until stiff. Gradually pour hot syrup over egg whites, beating constantly. Beat for three minutes. Reduce speed to low and gradually beat in confectioners' sugar. Beat on high speed for five minutes.

*High ratio shortening is manufactured specifically for icings and cakes. Gives better results than general purpose shortening. Available at cake decorating supply outlets.

Cake Trimmings & Egg Yolks

When you're finished trimming the cake, what do you do with the leftover pieces? And what about the egg yolks you've saved from the icing recipes! Following are some great ideas for utilizing those leftovers you don't want to waste.

Layer trimmings in parfait glasses with gelatin, pudding, pie filling, fresh fruit or ice cream.

Layer large trimmings in a small cake pan. Drizzle thinned Buttercream Icing between layers. Freeze and cut into squares. Serve with ice cream or chocolate topping.

For a delicious torte, layer slices of trimmings or crumbs with coconut and chocolate flavoring over the layers. Make as many layers as trimmings allow. Allow mixture to set up before slicing. Serve with ice cream.

Cancoos Combine cake crumbs with Buttercream Icing and stir until mixture can be easily handled. Stir in nuts, raisins, dates, coconut or miniature marshmallows. Lightly flour hands and roll mixture into balls. Place on baking sheets and flatten slightly. Allow to dry for one hour. Dip in chocolate flavoring.

Unbaked Cookies

    2 cups finely crumbled cake crumbs
    ½ cup Buttercream Icing (more as needed)
    2 tablespoons semisweet chocolate pieces
    2 tablespoons flaked coconut
    2 tablespoons chopped nuts
    2 tablespoons finely chopped maraschino cherries
    16 miniature marshmallows
    ¼ teaspoon vanilla
    1 tablespoon meringue powder
       Graham cracker crumbs or chocolate
       flavored coating

Combine all ingredients and mix thoroughly. Form into a long roll. Roll in graham cracker crumbs. Chill and slice.

Variation: Rather than rolling in graham cracker crumbs, chill the roll for 1 hour, then slice and dip in melted chocolate flavored coating.

Egg Yolk Noodles

    ½ cup egg yolks
    ½ teaspoon salt
    ½ cup half and half
    2 cups plus 2 tablespoons flour

Combine egg yolks, salt and half and half in a large mixing bowl. Add half of the flour and mix well. Add more of the flour and stir until mixture is too thick to stir. Work remaining flour in with hands. Place dough on a lightly floured surface. Roll out until dough is very thin. Place uncut dough on baking sheets and bake for five minutes at 275°, turning once. Immediately cut into strips the desired width.

Deluxe Lemon Dessert

    ½   cup egg yolks
    ½   cup lukewarm water
    ⅛   teaspoon baking soda
    1   cup granulated sugar
    1½ cups cake flour
    ½   teaspoon salt
    2   teaspoons baking powder
    1   teaspoon vanilla

Combine egg yolks, water and soda in a large bowl and beat until very foamy. Gradually add sugar and mix well. Sift dry ingredients together. Carefully fold dry ingredients into egg mixture. Fold in vanilla. Bake at 350° in an ungreased tube pan for forty-five minutes. Invert pan and allow to cool completely. Remove from pan and cut crosswise into three layers. Fill with Lemon Filling and frost with a white frosting.

Lemon Filling

    ¾   cup granulated sugar
    3   tablespoons cornstarch
    ¼   teaspoon salt
    ¾   cup water
    1   tablespoon butter
    2   tablespoons grated lemon rind
    ⅓   cup lemon juice

Combine sugar, cornstarch and salt in a small saucepan. Gradually stir in water. Bring to a boil, stirring constantly. Boil for one minute. Remove from heat. Stir in butter and lemon rind. Gradually stir in lemon juice. Cool thoroughly.

Lesson 1
Icing the Cake

1. Cool cake layers completely.
2. Use a cake plate or a cardboard circle at least 1 inch larger in diameter than the cake and cover it with a doily.
3. Place one layer, top side up, in the center of doily or plate.
   Note At this point the cake may be placed on a turntable or lazy susan to facilitate icing.
4. Trim cake with a knife to level it, if necessary. (Fig. 1)
5. Spread a generous amount of Buttercream Icing (recipe on page 4) on the bottom layer, to within one-half inch of the edge. (Fig. 2)
6. Level the top of the next layer, if necessary.
7. Place top layer of cake, cut side down, on the icing.
   Note The top layer will slide easily into place if the icing dries a little to form a light crust before the top is added. If the top layer is positioned while the icing is soft, it cannot be moved.
8. Crumb ice the cake by spreading a thin layer of icing on the sides of the cake, using long strokes of a spatula held perpendicular to the cake. (Fig. 3)
9. Frost the top of the cake, sealing in any loose crumbs.
10. Frost roughly after the icing has formed a crust, first on the sides, then on top. Use long, firm strokes to smooth the icing. Remove any excess icing with the spatula. (Fig. 4)

Note If the cake is on a turntable, the sides can be frosted in one smooth motion, holding the spatula perpendicular to the turntable as it rotates. To frost the top, hold the spatula parallel to the turntable as it rotates.

If the icing is not smooth, use one of the following methods to obtain a smooth finish:

Method 1
Dip a long spatula into hot water and smooth the icing with long strokes.

Method 2
Allow the icing to dry slightly. Place a strip of waxed paper against the cake and lightly press back and forth against the cake until the surface is smooth. To achieve a pebbled effect, use textured paper toweling instead of waxed paper.

Fig. 1

Fig. 2

Fig. 3

Fig. 4

Clockwise from the top
Snowberry Cake Berries and top border, #4 tube; leaves and bottom border, #352 tube
Forsythia Cake Borders and stems, #4 tube; flowers, #16 tube
Hyacinth Cake Bowl, #4 tube; filled in and smoothed with a spatula and water; flowers, #16 tube; border leaves, #352 tube; flower leaves, cut parchment cone; bottom border, #4 tube

The Importance of Practice

The importance of practice cannot be emphasized enough. Cake decorating is an acquired skill, and practice is essential to perfect it.

To practice you will need a practice board. Practice boards can be made of several things: formica sawed to a convenient size, the back of a baking sheet, a smooth plastic placemat or cardboard covered with dark adhesive paper. Practice boards can also be purchased from cake decorating supply outlets.

Practice decorating using Buttercream Icing (recipe on page 4). Make a supply of icing and store it at room remperature. After the icing has been used to practice, scrape it up with a knife and return it to the decorating bag or a container. As a beginning decorator, use only a small amount of icing at a time.

Set aside thirty minutes each day to perfect the techniques described, and practice faithfully. You will be amazed at the progress you make from day to day.

Lesson 2
Bulb Work, Stems, Leaves, Star Tubes

Pressure control is a very important part of cake decorating, and practicing bulb work will lay the foundation for expert results. Bulb work is important because it is the basis of figure piping and many of the borders.

To practice bulb work you will need
#4 tube
Boiled, Royal or Buttercream Icing

How to Do Bulb Work
1. Fill the bag half full of icing; fold top down securely.
2. Hold the bag perpendicular to the practice board, tube raised slightly above the board.
3. Apply pressure to the bag. As the ball of icing increases in size, raise the tube slightly, keeping it pressed lightly into the ball of icing.
4. When the ball of icing is the desired size, release pressure, pause momentarily, and remove the tube from the icing. (Fig. 1)

Practice making balls of uniform size, increasing and decreasing pressure to achieve the desired size. Avoid points on tops of balls.

Elongated Shapes
To make an elongated shape you will need
#4 tube

How to make an elongated shape
1. Begin with a ball; then move the tube from the perpendicular position to a 45° angle, applying steady pressure. Continue to move smoothly until the desired length is obtained. (Fig. 2)

Stems
To make stems you will need
Green Buttercream Icing thinned with a small amount of water
Parchment bag with a small opening or a #1 or #2 writing tube

How to make a stem
1. Hold the tube at a 45° angle. (Fig. 3, p. 9)
2. Touch the practice board at the top of the stem line, apply pressure, and raise the tube, allowing the stem to curve and fall into place. *Note* Do not form stems directly on the cake, allowing the tube to touch the cake. This will cause a rough, uneven line.

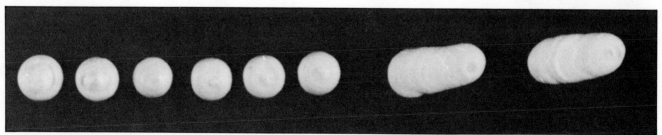

Fig. 1/Bulb work   Fig. 2/Elongated shapes

Leaves

To make leaves you will need
Leaf tube or parchment cone cut ∧

Leaves are made using the inverted "V" tube or a parchment cone that is cut into an inverted V. Leaf tube numbers, from smallest to largest, are 349, 350 and 352.

How to cut a parchment bag into an inverted "V" (∧)
1. Fill the bag half full of icing; fold top down securely.
2. Force icing into the point of the bag.
3. Press the point flat.
4. Cut a ∧ as shown. (Diag. A)

How to make a leaf
1. Hold the tube or parchment cone at a 45° angle. (Fig. 3)
2. Holding the bag steady, apply pressure until the desired width is achieved.
3. Reduce pressure and pull the tube up to make a point. (Fig. 4)

Note To make a textured leaf, use a slight jiggling motion as pressure is released.

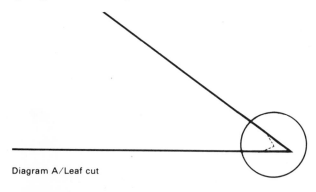
Diagram A/Leaf cut

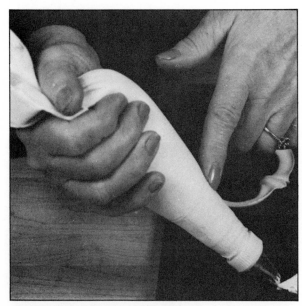
Fig. 3/Holding the bag at a 45° angle

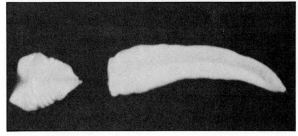

#16 Star tube   Fig. 5/Stars

Fig. 4/Leaves

Star Tubes

One of the most useful tubes is the star tube, which is available in various sizes with an open or almost closed tip. For general border work, use a #32 tube for large stars, a #16 for small stars.

How to make a star (Fig. 5)
1. Hold the tube perpendicular to the practice board.
2. Apply slight pressure, just enough to allow the points of the star to show around the edge of the tube.
3. Release pressure, pull the tube straight up.

Snowberries
(See cake on page 7.)

To make snowberries you will need
#4 writing tube, brown icing
Leaf tube, dark green icing
Small writing tube, white icing
Black food coloring

How to make snowberries
1. Frost the cake a light green.
2. Use brown icing with the #4 tube to make shallow S-curved stems crossing over the cake top.
3. Cover the stems with dark green leaves using a leaf tube, spacing the leaves irregularly.
4. Use the writing tube and white icing to form clusters of small white berries.
5. After the berries have dried slightly, use a toothpick to place a tiny dot of black food color on each berry.

Cattails

To make cattails you will need
Writing tube, green icing
#4 tube, brown icing
Leaf tube, green icing

How to make cattails

1. Using green icing, form clusters of moderately long stems, some straight and some slightly curved.
2. Using bulb work technique and brown icing with a #4 tube, move the tube slowly over the stem, applying even pressure, until the length of the cattail is completed.
   Note Keep the end of the tube under the surface of the icing as the cattail is formed.
3. Add thin, elongated leaves to finish. (Fig. 1)

Forsythia

(See cake on page 7.)

To make forsythia you will need
#4 writing tube, brown icing
#16 or other star tube, yellow icing

How to make forsythia

1. Make a bush of brown branches using the stem technique.
2. Cover the branches with clusters of tiny yellow stars, allowing some of the brown stems to show through. (Fig. 2)

Hyacinths (Fig. 3)

(See cake on page 7.)
This flower incorporates stems, leaves and stars.

To make a hyacinth you will need
#1 or #2 tube or a cut parchment bag, green icing
#16 tube, icing in desired color
Leaf tube, green icing, or parchment bag cut
  ∧, green icing

How to make a hyacinth

1. Make a short green stem using a #1 or #2 tube or cut parchment bag.
2. Form three rows of tiny stars at the top of the stem with the #16 tube. The middle row should be slightly higher than the first and last.
3. Make a row of tiny stars directly on top of the middle row, but one star less at the top.
4. Tuck very tiny stars at an angle alongside each star of the middle row to give it a rounded effect.
5. Add two curving, elongated leaves on each side of the stem, using a leaf tube or cut parchment bag. Make one leaf slightly longer than the other.

Fig. 1/Cattails

Fig. 2/Forsythia

Fig. 3/Hyacinth

Sweet Pea Cake (Happy Birthday Peggy) Stems, border trim and writing, #4 tube; sweet peas, #104 tube; borders, #16 tube
Run Sugar Cake (Happy Birthday Jenny) Little girl, run sugar, details painted with food color; tree trunk, writing and swing, #4 tube; leaves, cut parchment cone; sweet pea clusters, #104 tube; shell border, #32 tube (Pattern by Ginger Roth)

Lesson 3
Fan Petals, Sweet Peas, Basic Borders

Fan Petals

Except for the star, the fan shape is used more than any other pattern in cake decorating. Practice making fan petals before proceeding with the flowers described below.

To make fan petals you will need
Flower Decorator Icing
Decorating bag
#104 tube

How to make fan petals
1. Place the wide end of the tube against the surface of the practice board, the narrow end raised slightly and pointed to the left.
2. Starting with the tube angled to the left, apply pressure and then swivel the tube to the right, keeping the wide end down against the board and the narrow end raised slightly.
3. Keeping pressure steady, release with a sharp, upward pull to finish. (Fig. 1)

Sweet Pea Number 1
(See cake on page 10.)
To make sweet peas you will need
Royal Icing
#104 tube

This sweet pea is usually made in clusters and makes good fill-ins used with other flowers. They are pink, lavender or white, but artistic license can be used to make them any pastel color.

How to make sweet peas (Fig. 3)
1. Fill a bag half full of icing; fold corners in and the top down.
2. Stand the tube on end on the practice board, with the wide end lightly touching the surface.
3. Apply pressure, raising the tube slightly off the practice board.
4. Maintain steady pressure and bring the tube back down to the same point, releasing pressure with a sharp, upward pull.
   Note Pressure applied while the tube is slightly off the surface will cause this petal to ruffle slightly.
5. Hold the tube with the wide end in the same position as the first petal was started, but point the narrow end slightly to the left.
6. Apply pressure, raise the tube, and then lower it to the same position, releasing pressure as the tube comes back down.
7. Start the third petal with the wide end in the same position as the first, but with the narrow end pointed to the right. Apply pressure and raise the tube slightly. Bring the tube down, releasing pressure as it returns to the starting point.

To make these in quantity for later use in clusters, attach a large piece of waxed paper to a flat surface with dots of icing. Make the sweet peas in rows on waxed paper and allow them to dry. Store, covered, in a dry place until ready to use.

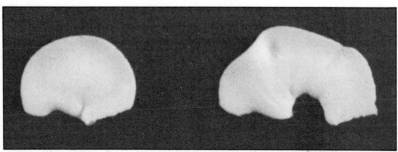

Fig. 1/Right way to make a fan petal   Fig. 2/Wrong way to make a fan petal

Fig. 3/Sweet pea Number 1

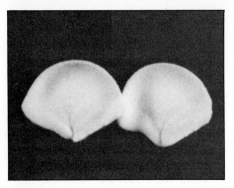

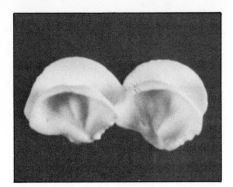

Fig. 4/Step 1 of Sweet Pea Number 2

Fig. 5/Step 2

Fig. 6/Steps 3, 4 and 5

Sweet Peas Number 2
(See cake on page 10.)

To make sweet peas you will need
Flower Decorator Icing
#104 tube

How to make sweet peas
1. Make two fan petals side by side and parallel to each other. Ruffle the petals slightly by applying extra pressure as the tube is swiveled. (Fig. 4)
2. Make two smaller fan petals on top of the first two, but raise the narrow end of the tube slightly, so that these petals will stand up over the first petals and will not lie flat against them. These petals should also ruffle slightly. (Fig. 5)
3. Make small center petals by standing the tube on end, beginning at the top where the second set of fan petals come together. Form the stand-up petal in an arch from the top to the bottom. Keep the tube just above the petals. (Fig. 6)
4. Make one small petal arched to the right and another petal arched to the left to create an oblong opening between, but not at the ends of, the small petals.

5. Tuck a small amount of green icing around the base of the flower.
6. Use a #1 tube to add a curving stem and curling tendrils.

Shell Border
(See cakes on pages 10, 14, 19, 23, 26, 30, 39, 42, 55)

To make a shell border you will need
Buttercream, Boiled or Royal Icing.
#32 star tube or other star tube

The shell is the most commonly used border, so practice to perfect it. Although any star tube can be used, the #32 tube makes lovely shell borders.

How to make a shell border (See Fig. 7)
1. Hold tube at a 45° angle. Apply pressure, keeping the tip of the tube slightly under the surface of the icing, pushing up and back slightly into the shell as it builds up.
2. Pull the tube down and out as pressure is released.
3. Begin the next shell near the end of the last one.
4. Repeat the above process, pushing back gently into the shell as it builds up, until it barely covers the tail of the last shell.

Fig. 7/Shell Border

Fig. 8/C-Scroll Border

Fig. 1/Scroll Border

Fig. 2/Reverse Scroll Border

C-Scroll Border

(See cake on page 19.)

To make a C-scroll border you will need
Buttercream, Boiled or Royal Icing.
#16 star tube

How to make a C-scroll border (Fig. 8, p. 13)

1. Hold the tube nearly upright. Apply pressure and form a C ending with a curved tail.
2. Continue by backing up a little into the curve of the last tail, then moving forward to form the next C. Make in one continuous motion.

Scroll Border

To make a scroll border you will need
Buttercream, Boiled or Royal Icing.
#16 star tube or other small star tube

How to make a scroll border (See Fig. 1)

1. Hold the tube nearly upright. Apply a great deal of pressure and form a question mark.

2. Complete the tail of the question mark. Do not release pressure. Begin the next question mark, fitting the top curve into the tail of the preceding question mark.

Reverse Scroll Border

(See cake on page 46.)

To make a reverse scroll you will need
Buttercream, Boiled or Royal Icing.
#16 star tube or other small star tube

How to make a reverse scroll border (Fig. 2.)

1. Hold the tube nearly upright. Apply a great deal of pressure and make a script letter *e*, first right side up and then upside down. (Diag. 1). Do not release pressure. Continue until border is completed.

Diag. 1/Pattern for reverse scroll border

Lesson 4
Flower Nail and Roses

The Flower Nail

Some flowers can either be made directly on the cake or prepared in advance on a flower nail. Flower nails are available in several sizes and shapes. We will be using the #1, #7, #9 or #12 nail during the course of this book.

How to use the flower nail

1. Hold the nail with the thumb and first finger of the left hand and lightly steady it between the fourth and fifth fingers. (Fig. 1, p. 16) The head of the nail should rest against the side of

the finger at all times; the tip is held steady by placing the little finger over it.

2. Roll the nail between the first joint of the first finger and the end of that finger. The finger will bend or arch as the nail almost reaches the end of the finger. The finger should quickly and lightly straighten itself. (Reverse the entire procedure if you are left-handed.)

Practice rolling the nail until the action becomes smooth, steady and comfortable.

Chocolate Cake Shell borders, #32 tube; roses, #104 tube; stems, writing and leaves, cut parchment cone

Poppy Cake (Happy Father's Day) Bottom shell border, #32 tube; top rope border, #16 tube; side drop border, #16 tube; poppies, #104 tube; writing, leaves and stems, #4 tube

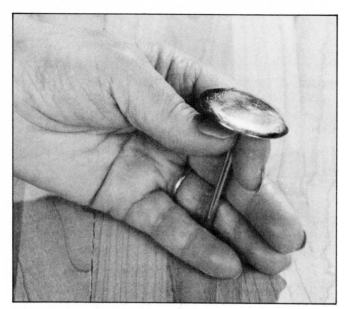
Fig. 1/Holding the flower nail

How to make flowers on the nail

1. Cut waxed paper into 1½-inch squares. (Ready-cut squares with guidelines are available at cake decorating supply outlets.) The squares should be no larger than 1½ inches, or they will interfere with the formation of the flowers.
2. Place a dot of icing on the nail to hold the waxed paper in place. Attach the waxed paper.
3. Make a flower as described in the following lessons.
4. Slip the waxed paper and flower off the nail.
5. Place on a tray or baking sheet to dry.

Drying Flowers

Most flowers are easily handled if they are dried before they are used. Flowers made of Royal Icing will usually dry in about twenty-four hours at room temperature; flowers made of Flower Decorator Icing require about two days to dry completely.

The drying process is often affected by humid weather conditions and must be taken into consideration when deciding how far in advance flowers must be made. When humid conditions prevail, drying is prolonged. Household air conditioners alleviate this problem somewhat by removing humidity from the air.

Flowers made of Royal Icing can be oven dried quickly, but they must be watched carefully. Preheat the oven to 100°, or until barely warm. Place the flowers, still on the waxed paper squares, on a baking sheet. Place the baking sheet in the oven. Watch closely. If one area is drying more rapidly than another, turn the baking sheet around. When the tops are dried, carefully remove the waxed paper and turn the flowers over to dry the undersides.

Do *not* attempt to oven dry flowers made of Flower Decorator Icing. Because shortening is used in this icing, the flowers will melt.

Roses
(See cakes on pages 14 and 26.)
Roses can be made with the following tubes: 101s, #101, #102, #103, #104, #124, #125, #126, #127, #127D, #128. Tubes #97, #116, #117, #118, and #119 are used to make roses with very curved petals. The most commonly used rose tube is #104.

To make a rose you will need
Flower Decorator or Royal Icing
Waxed paper squares
Coupler
#8 tube
#7 nail
#104 tube

How to make a rose
1. Attach coupler and #8 tube to decorating bag. Fill with icing.
2. Place a few waxed paper squares on the practice board, securing each with a dot of icing.
3. Form a ½-inch ball of icing in the center of a square, keeping the tip of the tube slightly under the surface of the icing. Bring the tube straight up about 1 inch from the ball of icing

Fig. 2　　　Fig. 3　　　Fig. 4　　　Fig. 5

to form a cone. Release pressure gradually as the tube moves upward. (Fig. 2, p. 16) Bring the tip of the tube out of the icing as the cone is completed.

4. Change to the #104 tube.
5. Place a dot of icing on the nail. Place the cone of icing on the waxed paper on the nail.
6. Holding the nail in the left hand, lightly place the wide end of the tube just below the top center of the cone of icing.
7. While rolling the nail counterclockwise, apply pressure and form the center, tipping the tube slightly inward so the second cone will have a small center hole at the top. (Fig. 3). Release pressure and break off.
8. Add three overlapping petals, each of which should cover about one-half of the center of the rose. To do this press the wide end of the tube lightly against the icing at the base of the cone, close to the nail, pointing the narrow end to the right. Apply pressure and turn the narrow end upward, close to the cone, then to the left and down almost to the nail, arching the icing to form a petal.(Fig. 4)
9. Bring the tube back slightly to overlap the first petal. Again, arch the icing up and to the left. Repeat for the third petal.
10. Add five more petals using the above procedure, again starting at the base of the flower, close to the nail. Tip the narrow end of the tube out further to form a more open petal which will roll at the top. (Fig. 5)
11. Slip the waxed paper with the completed rose onto a tray to dry.

Note This flower may be made directly on the nail without the waxed paper and placed on the cake. (Fig. 6) Slip the tips of partially opened shears under the completed rose and remove it from the nail with the points. Place the rose on the cake by closing the shears and sliding it into place with the end of the flower nail.

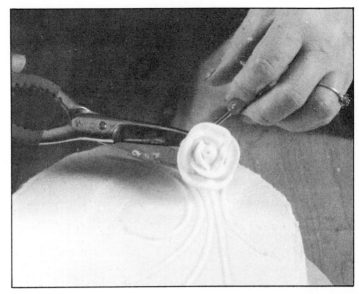
Fig. 6/Removing the rose from the nail with shears

Laydown Rose and Rosebud
(See cake on page 42.)

To make a laydown rose and rosebud you will need
Pink Flower Decorator or Royal Icing
#104 tube
Writing tube, green icing

How to make a laydown rose
(See cake on page 42.)
Note All petals of this flower start at the same point.

1. Make a fan petal. (See FAN PETALS, page 9.) (Fig. 7)
2. Place the wide end of the tube at the center of the base of the fan petal, the narrow end at a 45° angle, and pointed slightly to the left. Move the tube slightly off the fan petal and up toward the tip of the fan petal, swiveling the tube slightly to the right as it returns to the base. The tube should be nearly perpendicular to the base as it comes

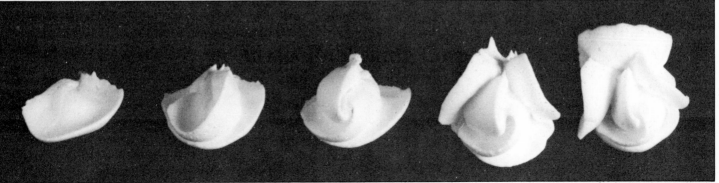

Fig. 7   Fig. 8   Fig. 9   Fig. 10   Fig. 11

back down. This petal should be a little higher and more elongated than the fan petal, with the right side definitely standing away from the fan petal. (Fig. 8, p. 17.)

3. Touch the right back side of the second petal with the tube. Pipe a small amount of icing to make this petal roll into a rose center. Immediately pull the tube toward the bottom of the petal, releasing pressure and giving a sharp pull to break off the icing. (Fig. 9)

4. Place the wide end of the tube at the base of the flower, tucked as close as possible between the fan petal and the rose center. Tip the narrow end out slightly. Apply pressure, arching the petal up and toward you, wrapping half of the center bud on one side. Repeat the procedure, wrapping the other side of the bud with an arched petal, over-lapping the preceding petal slightly. (Fig. 10)

5. The last petal is a fan petal. Place the wide end of the tube against the center bottom point of the flower, pointing the narrow end to the left. Apply pressure, swiveling the tube from left to right, keeping the wide end in the center, but letting it rise a little and then come back down. (Fig. 11)

6. Use a writing tube to add green sepals. Start each sepal at the center base of the flower using heavy pressure, and decreasing pressure as sepals are placed around the petals. Tip the ends out slightly as pressure is released and break off the icing.

7. Still using the writing tube, add a small ball of green icing at the center base of the flower, then a curved stem.

Rosebuds
To make a rosebud, complete steps 2 and 3 only.

Lesson 5
Chrysanthemums, Basket Weaving, Grapes, More Borders

Chrysanthemum
(See cake on opposite page)
To make chrysanthemums you will need
Flower Decorator or Royal Icing
Food coloring: yellow, gold, rust, or lavender
1½-inch Waxed paper squares
#7 Flower nail
#79, #80 or #81 tube

How to make chrysanthemums
1. Attach a square of waxed paper to the nail with a dot of icing.
2. Make a ball of icing in the center of the waxed paper. (Fig. 1, p. 20)
3. Hold the tube parallel to the nail head and insert the tube, curved end down, slightly into the bottom of the icing ball. Apply pressure and bring the tube out, pulling out a pointed petal. (Fig. 2) Turn nail and repeat, making a row of petals around the bottom.
   Note All petals should rest on the foundation ball, not on each other.
4. Tip the tube up slightly to make the second row of pointed petals. (Fig. 3) Make rows of petals until the ball of icing is completely covered.
5. Tip the tube up more for each row. (Fig. 4) To form the center petals, hold the tube perpendicular to the nail head. (Fig. 5)

Clockwise from the top
Mum Cake Mums, #80 tube; basket, #233 tube; zig zag borders, #16 tube; shell border, #32 tube; leaves and stems, cut parchment cone; cattails, #4 tube
Grape Cake Cornucopia, #32 tube; grapes, #4 tube; top border, #16 tube; zig zag bottom border, #32 tube
Daisy Cake Daisies, #104 and #233 tubes; stems, writing, leaves, and drop side border, #4 tube; top border, #16 tube; bottom border, #32 tube

Top Row/Fig. 1-3
Bottom Row/Fig. 4-5

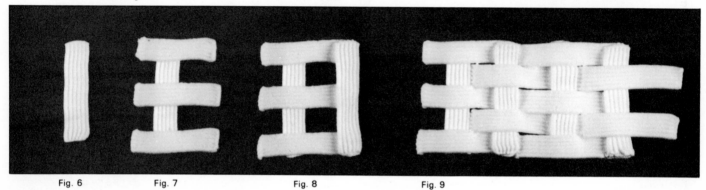

Fig. 6   Fig. 7   Fig. 8   Fig. 9

Basket Weaving
To basket weave you will need
Icing firm enough to hold pattern lines
#4, #16, #46, #46°, #47, #48 or any star tube

How to basket weave
1. Make a vertical line to the depth of the area to be covered, e. g. the whole side of a cake, or a basket shape on top. (Fig. 6)
2. Make horizontal lines over the vertical line, allowing a space the width of the tube between each horizontal line. (Fig. 7)
3. Cover ends on the right side of the horizontal line with another vertical line. (Fig. 8)
4. Make horizontal lines, starting against the first vertical line and filling in between the horizontal lines, bringing the icing over the second vertical line. (Fig. 9)
5. Add the next vertical line, covering the ends of the horizontal lines.
6. Repeat as needed to complete.

Grapes
(See cake on page 19.)
To make grapes you will need
Buttercream or any soft icing that will hold its shape
#4 or other writing tube

To make grapes
1. Make a V-shaped base using a circular or back and forth motion. (Fig. 10)
2. Beginning a little below the bottom point of the V make small balls, bringing the tail of each ball down. (Fig. 11) Each tail will be covered with the next ball. Cover the entire base, placing balls irregularly, not in rows.
3. Add grapes to the top to give it a rounded effect. Tail should not show. (Fig. 12)
4. Make a stem with a curling tendril attached.
5. Place three small leaves close together to form a large grape leaf and attach it to the stem.

Fig. 10-12

Rope Border

(See cake on page 14.)

To make a rope border you will need
Buttercream or Boiled Icing
#32 or other star tube

Hold to make a rope border

1. Make a slightly curved letter S, holding the tube at a 40° angle. (Fig. 13)
2. Reach under the icing with the tip of the tube. Apply minimal pressure, pull the tube down, and then lift the icing over the right end of the S, forming the next S.
3. Continue making the border around the cake. *Note* Maintain gentle but steady pressure so that each section is uniform.

Swag Border (Fig. 1, p. 22)

To make a swag border you will need
Buttercream or Boiled Icing
#104 tube

How to make a swag border

1. Mark the side of the cake in even sections. To do so, cut a piece of waxed paper the same size as the cake top. Fold paper into eighths.
2. Lay the paper on the cake. Using a spatula, make a slight mark at each fold.
3. Begin the first swag on the left side of one of the sections. Place the wide end of the tube up and barely against the cake; the narrow end tipped slightly.
4. Apply pressure and arch the swag down to the right and then up in a quick, smooth motion until it reaches the end of the section.

Zig Zag Swag

(See cakes on page 23. Examples of straight zig zag border are on pages 10, 14, and 51.)

To make a zig zag swag you will need
Buttercream or Boiled Icing
#16 or other small star tube

How to make a zig zag swag

1. Mark the cake into sections. (See SWAG BORDER above.)
2. Begin the first swag on the left side of one of the sections. Apply pressure, moving the tube up and down slightly to form a rippled swag.
3. Arch the swag down and then up until it reaches the end of the sections. (Fig. 14)

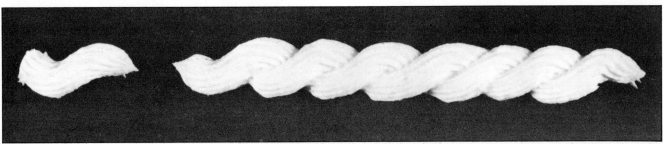

Fig. 13

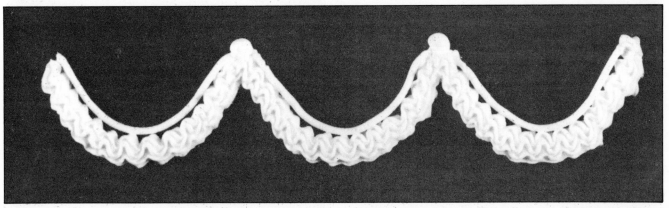

Fig. 14

Fig. 1

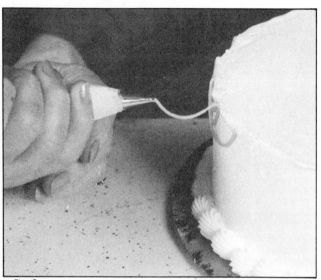

Fig. 2

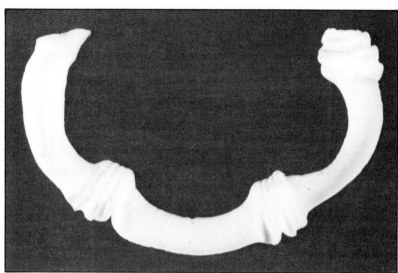

Fig. 3

Drop or String Work

(See cakes on pages 19, 26, 51, 55, and 58.)

String work piped over any of the garlands adds a decorative touch to the border.

To form strings you will need

Boiled or Royal Icing or Buttercream that has been mixed with corn syrup (1 teaspoon corn syrup to 2 cups icing)

#4 tube

How to make strings

1. Lightly touch the side of the cake with the tube, holding the tube as shown (Fig. 2)
2. Pull the icing toward you to the desired length, then swing it to the right and touch the string at the desired point.

Note Do not draw the string directly on the cake. Do not allow the tube to dip while pulling the string across.

Frame Border

(See cake on opposite page.)

To make a frame border you will need
#104 tube

How to make a frame border

1. Hold the tube nearly flat against the side of the cake, the wide end one-quarter inch from the outside top edge of the cake, the narrow end toward the outside edge and slightly raised.
2. Applying even pressure, make an arch, three short jiggles of the tube, another curve and three more jiggles. (Fig. 3)
3. Repeat until the cake is completely framed.

Bluebird Cake Birds, painted sugar mold; apple blossoms, (drop flowers) #190 tube; branches, #4 tube and cut parchment cone; leaves, leaf-cut parchment cone; background, scene painting; frame border, #104; top side and drop border, #16 tube; bottom border, #32 tube

Lesson 6
Piping Gel, Decorative Side Borders

Piping Gel

Piping gel is available clear and in colors. It is, however, more practical to purchase clear gel and add the desired food coloring as needed. Piping gel is too soft for flowers or borders and is best used for writing, water in scene painting, and church windows. A dot of colored gel between shells or scallops can accent borders on cake tops or sides. Simple designs, such as hearts, can also be piped with gel.

Church Windows
(See cake on page 46.)

To make church windows you will need
Piping gel colored as needed
Parchment bags for each color gel
Royal Icing

How to make church windows
1. Lightly sketch a stained glass window in the icing using a toothpick. (See cake on page 46.) Decide which colors will be used in each section. Avoid using the same color in adjoining sections.
2. Color piping gel as desired and fill parchment bags.
3. Cut small openings in the points of parchment bags.
4. Fill sections with gel using a dotting motion to achieve a bubbly effect.
5. Fill a parchment bag (or use a bag with a #1 tube) with black or gray Royal Icing and cut a small opening.
6. Outline each section and the outside of the window to simulate leading in stained-glass windows.

Decorative Side Borders
The following borders are based on a curved line.

To make the curved line you will need
Any icing soft enough to flow easily
#3 tube

How to make the curved line
1. Hold the tube at a 45° angle.
2. Apply pressure and move quickly to circle the cake with a smooth, flowing line.

Grape Border
(See cake on page 19.)

To make a grape border you will need
Buttercream Icing
#3 tube, green icing
#4 tube, purple icing
#350 tube, green icing
Parchment bag, green icing, with a very small opening cut in the end.

How to make a grape border
1. Make the basic curved line using the #3 tube and green icing.
2. Add various sizes of grape clusters using the #4 tube (see GRAPES, page 20), either following the line of the curve (Fig. 1) or hanging from each high and low point of the curve.
3. Add leaves as shown using the #350 tube.
4. Add curling tendrils and curved lines using the cut parchment bag.

Holly Border (Fig. 2)
(See cake on page 39.)

To make a holly border you will need
Buttercream Icing
#3 tube, green icing
#352 tube or parchment bag, green icing, cut ∧
#4 tube, red icing

How to make a holly border
1. Use the #3 tube to make the basic curved line around the cake.
2. Add a generous number of leaves to the line with the #352 tube or cut parchment bag. Tip some leaves up and some down, pointing all leaves in the same direction and spacing them irregularly.

Fig. 1

Fig. 2

3. Make two or three leaves, then lightly touch the edge of a leaf with a toothpick or the end of a flower nail. Do not push the toothpick into the icing. While the icing is still very soft, pull out small points along the edges of each leaf.

4. Pipe clusters of red berries at uneven intervals with the #4 tube. Vary the number of berries in each cluster.

Variation Use groupings of holly at 3 or 4 places in the center of the sides of a holiday cake. Make 2 holly leaves with the ends pointing out. Add a cluster of berries in the center where the leaves meet. (See cake on page 7.)

Writing
(See cakes on pages 35, 46, 55, and 62.)

To write you will need
Piping gel or any icing soft enough to flow easily
#1 tube or parchment bag cut with a small opening

How to write (Fig. 3)
1. Practice on waxed paper placed over lined paper until letters are even and of uniform thickness.
2. Hold the bag at the same angle a pencil is held. Apply steady pressure and write with a flowing line. Write as narrowly as possible. Add decorative flourishes, if desired.

Fig. 3

Lesson 7
Flowers, Beginning Figure Piping

Jonquil
(See cake on page 55.)

To make jonquils you will need
Flower Decorator or Royal Icing
Yellow food paste
Waxed paper squares
#7 flower nail
#104 tube, yellow icing
#4 tube, yellow icing
Parchment bag, yellow icing, cut with
 a small opening

How to make jonquils
1. Attach a square of waxed paper to the nail with a dot of icing.
2. Start with the wide end of the #104 tube at the center of the nail, the narrow end pointing slightly to the left and the tube at a 45° angle to the nail.
3. To make the first petal, apply pressure, sliding the tube to the outside edge of the nail. Turn the nail slightly and slide the tube back to the center. Make sure that the icing comes together in the center of the petal. (Fig. 1)
4. Add a second petal opposite the first, using the above technique.
5. Add four more petals, spacing them between the first two.

6. Use the #4 tube to make a small ball in the center of the petals. (Fig. 2)
7. Make the trumpet by using the #4 tube and circling the outside edge of the ball and then the outside edge of the trumpet, so that it is wide at the top and narrow at the bottom.
8. Jiggle the parchment bag around the top of the trumpet to form a small ruffled edge. (Fig. 3)
9. Use a fine artist's brush to add a small amount of yellow paste to the ruffled edge. (Fig. 4)
10. Pinch each petal lightly to point the ends. If the icing sticks to your fingers, coat them with cornstarch.

Pansies
(See cake on page 55.)
   The pansy can be made completely in yellow Royal Icing, dried, and painted with a very fine brush using paste food colors.

To make pansies you will need
Yellow Royal or Flower Decorator Icing
Waxed paper squares
Purple or violet food color
Parchment cone
#7 nail
#104 tube

Fig. 1-4

Baby Sheet Cake Borders, #16 tube; background, scene painting; stork and booties, #4 tube and cut parchment cone
Mother's Day Cake Cameo, painted chocolate mold; roses, #104 tube; borders, #32 tube; writing, drop work and top trim, #2 tube

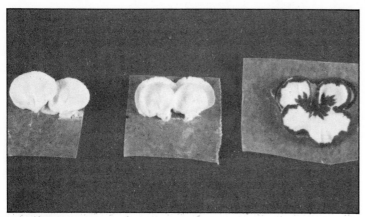

Fig. 1-3

How to make a pansy

1. Attach a waxed paper square to the nail with a dot of icing.
2. Insert the #104 tube into a parchment cone.
3. Use a small brush and the paste color, and, starting inside at the tube, paint a stripe halfway up the inside of the parchment cone. Paint another stripe directly opposite the first.
4. Fill the cone half full of icing and fold down the top.
5. Turn the tube so the color stripes are positioned one at the narrow end and one at the wide end of the tube.
6. Make two fan petals, side by side, on the top half of the nail. (Fig. 1)
7. Tip the narrow end of the tube up slightly and form two more fan petals directly on top of the first two petals but slightly smaller. If the colored stripes have been positioned correctly, there will be purple edges on the petals and purple in the center of the flower.
8. Position the wide end of the tube in the center of the nail where the petals come together. Hold the tube just above the nail with the narrow end a little higher than the wide end.
9. Overlap the last petal slightly, keep the wide end in the same spot, and swivel the nail, using a great deal of pressure, to make a ruffled petal.
10. Bring the tube up perpendicular to the nail so it does not touch the petals already made, and end the petal just over the petal on the left side of the flower.

Booties
(See color photo on page 26.)

To make booties you will need
Buttercream Icing
#4 or any writing tube
#1 tube

How to make a bootie
1. Position the tube perpendicular to the practice board. Form a ball, keeping the tip of the tube under the surface of the icing, applying pressure until the ball reaches the desired height for the toe of the bootie. (Fig. 4)
2. Move the tube slowly backward, keeping a steady pressure so that the height remains the same. (Fig. 5)
3. When the desired length is reached, build the icing straight up from the bootie, then pipe two rows of icing around the outside edge of the ankle. (Fig. 6)
4. Trim the booties using a #1 tube to make a bow on the toe and a fine zig zag line around the top of the ankle in a contrasting color of icing.
5. Make booties in pairs.

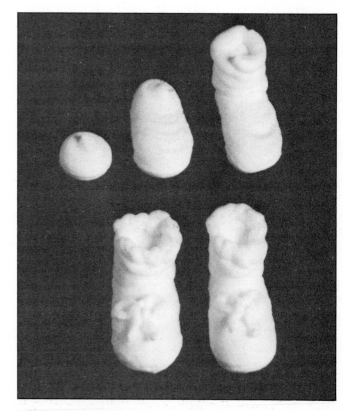

Top Row/Fig. 4-6
Bottom Row/Completed booties

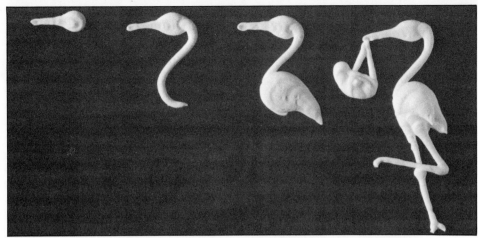

Fig. 1-4

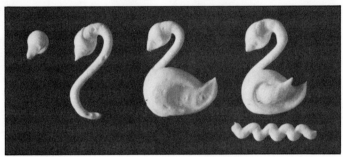

Fig. 5-8

Storks

To make a stork you will need
Softened Buttercream or Boiled Icing
#4 tube

How to make a stork
1. Form a ball for the head. (Fig. 1)
2. Push the tube into the icing and apply slight pressure to pull out a long beak from the side of the head. (Fig. 1)
3. Push the tube into the side of the head opposite the bill, and apply pressure to form a long, graceful neck. (Fig. 2)
4. Build a ball into the lower curve of the neck, using a great deal of pressure and keeping the tube under the surface of the icing. (Fig. 3)
5. Elongate the ball and tip it downward, releasing the pressure to form the tail. (Fig. 3)
6. Push the tube into the center of the body and pull out a wing which dips downward slightly. (Fig. 4)
7. Add two long, thin legs, one of them bent forward. (Fig. 4) Make the legs slightly heavy in the thighs and thin to the knee; then add knobby knees and finish with thin lower legs and feet.
8. Pipe a bundle which appears to have a baby inside. (Fig. 4) (You may also use a small plastic baby and cover all but the head with icing.)

Swans

Swans are lovely on petit fours or cupcakes. Larger swans are beautiful in water scenes on cake tops. Small ones can be used as part of a side border on wedding cakes.

To make a swan you will need
Softened Buttercream or Boiled Icing
#4 tube

How to make a swan
1. Form a ball for the head (Fig. 5)
2. Hold the tube at a 45° angle and pull a beak downward from the head. (Fig. 5)
3. Push the tube into the top of the head and, using heavy pressure, form a graceful S-curved neck. (Fig. 6)
4. Form a body, starting at the lower end of the neck and fitting the curved front of the body into the lower curve of the swan's neck. Build the body backwards, using heavy pressure and keeping the tube under the surface of the icing. (Fig. 7)
5. As the body builds backwards, bring the tube downward and then release pressure, pulling the tube upward to form a tail. (Fig. 7)
6. Push the tube slightly into the center of the body, and apply pressure to pull out a wing. (Fig. 8)
7. Add a short wave of water under the swan and an eye, if desired. (Fig. 8)

Lesson 8
More Figure Piping

Bells
To make bells you will need
Buttercream Icing
#4 or other writing tube

How to make bells
1. Make a small ball of icing with the #4 tube, keeping the end of the tube under the surface of the icing. (Fig. 1)
2. Build around the outside edge of the ball, making a circular motion, gradually increasing the size as you build the bell outward, keeping the tube under the surface of the icing. (Fig. 2 and 3)
3. Add a small ball to the inside of the bell for a clapper.(Fig. 4)

Palm Tree (Fig. 5)
To make a palm tree you will need
#4 tube, brown icing
#350 tube, green icing, or parchment bag, green icing, cut ∧

How to make a palm tree
1. Form the trunk by making a circular motion, keeping the tube under the surface of the icing. Build from the top of the trunk to the base. Curve the trunk slightly.
2. Form fronds by using the #350 tube and green icing or the cut parchment bag. (The tube will make a thicker leaf than the parchment bag.) Fronds grow from the top of the tree, so start them all at the top. Each frond should curve up slightly and then tip downward.
3. Bring a few fronds straight out from the middle of the tree top and then let them tip downward.

Bare Tree or Tree with Foliage
#4 tube, soft brown icing
#352 tube, green icing, or cut parchment bag, green icing, cut ∧

How to make a bare tree (Fig. 6)
1. Use the #4 tube to form a trunk and the branches. Keep the icing rough to resemble tree bark.

How to make a tree with foliage
(See cake on page 10.)
1. Complete step 1 above.
2. Add clusters of small green leaves, allowing some of the branches to show through.

How to make a tree with autumn foliage
1. Complete step 1 under Bare Tree, above.
2. Use gold or red leaves in clusters on the tree.
   Note The tree on the Halloween cake on page 30 was made by forming the trunk around the curve of a round cake and extending the branches onto the cake top.

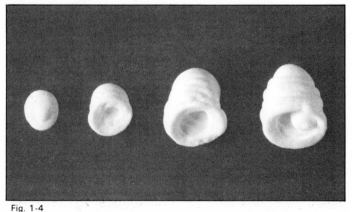

Fig. 1-4

Fig. 5

Fig. 6

Cowboy and Indian Cake Cowboy and Indian, painted chocolate molds; background, scene painting; pine tree and writing, cut parchment cones; other trees, #14 tube with soft icing; borders, #32 tube
Halloween Cake Background, scene painting; piping, #2, #4, and #6 tubes; borders, #16 and #32 tubes

Easy Shade Tree
To make an easy shade tree you will need
#4 tube, brown icing
#16 tube, green icing

How to make an easy shade tree (Fig. 1)
1. Use the #4 tube to make a short trunk. Add a small section of trunk and branches in the space above it.
2. Use the #16 tube and apply great pressure with a circular motion to make foliage, allowing some of the trunk and branches to show.

Cactus (Fig. 2)
(See cake on page 30.)
To make a cactus you will need
#16 tube, gray-green icing

How to make cactus
1. Make a straight line the desired height of the cactus.
2. Press the tube lightly into the line and applying pressure, pull straight out and then up to form branches. Place one or more branches irregularly on each side of the cactus.

Standing Evergreen or Christmas Tree (Fig. 3)
To make an evergreen or Christmas tree you will need
#352 tube, Green Royal Icing
Pointed ice cream cone or parchment cone, cut flat across open end

Ice cream cones are firmer to work with than parchment cones, but parchment cones can be made in different sizes. These trees can be made prior to Christmas and stored for later use. Make them in various sizes and use on a Christmas cake. Decorate with garlands, dragees or glitter.

How to make an evergreen or Christmas tree
1. Hold the cone with the left hand, inserting fingers inside the cone to support it.
2. Starting at the bottom of the cone, form leaves, pulling the points of the leaves downward. Complete a row and then continue upward, overlapping the leaves of the row below. (Fig. 1)
3. Complete the top by bringing three leaves together like a tent.
   Note A small amount of sifted confectioners' sugar sprinkled on while the icing is still soft will give the effect of snow.

Cornucopia
(See cake on page 19.)

To make a cornucopia you will need
Buttercream Icing
#16, #32, or any star tube

How to make a cornucopia
1. Begin at the small end of the cornucopia. Use a circular motion and heavy pressure, curving the end slightly and widening to form the opening.
2. Fill the opening with grapes, mums, or a combination of grapes and flowers, allowing them to spill out from the cornucopia onto the cake.

Fig. 1

Fig. 2

Fig. 3

Lesson 9
Scene Painting, Drop Flowers, Doll Cakes, Clowns

Scene Painting
(See cakes on pages 26 and 30.)

Almost any idea can be depicted in icing using cake decorating ability and a little imagination. Because the scene is on a cardboard that can be placed on the cake, the scene can be lifted from the cake and saved by the recipient. Scenes may also be created directly on the cake top.

To scene paint you will need
Boiled or Buttercream Icing
Cardboard circle cut to fit the cake top
Food coloring
Soft, 2-inch pastry brush
Parchment bags cut with small openings

How to scene paint
1. Ice the cardboard circle thinly.
2. Drop a very small amount of food coloring on the icing, for instance, blue for a sky in the upper area and blue and green for water in the lower area.
3. Dip a soft 2-inch pastry brush into water and shake off the excess moisture. Blend color into the icing unevenly. (Do not make the color even. The finished scene will look better if the color is unevenly blended.)
4. To make raised areas, such as mountains, hills, etc., use one of the following methods: (1) Paint the inside of a large parchment bag with the desired color and fill with white icing. Cut an opening and pipe the desired shapes. (2) Fill the bag with colored icing and pipe the desired areas and shapes.(3) Pipe the desired areas with white icing and blend in minute amounts of color with a brush and water.
5. Use smaller bags of colored icing to add features to the scene, such as swans on water, trees or shrubs on land, cacti, stones, etc., for a western scene.
6. Ice the cake and allow icing to dry thoroughly before positioning the cake board on the top.

Drop Flowers
(See cake on page 23.)

Easily made in a single motion, drop flowers are suitable for mass production.

To make drop flowers you will need
Royal Icing
#190 tube or any tube with a center nail or any star tube
Note If using a tube with a protruding center nail, cut the nail with wire cutters so that the nail is flush with the top of the tube.

How to make drop flowers
1. Fasten a sheet of waxed paper to a tray with several dots of icing.
2. Hold the bag and tube perpendicular to the tray, the tube perfectly flat against it. (Fig. 1)
3. Apply pressure, giving the tube a quarter turn.
4. Release pressure and raise the tube straight up with a slight jerk to break off.
5. Fill the sheet of waxed paper with drop flowers.
6. Finish flowers by putting several tiny dots of yellow icing in the center of each flower, or use a #233 tube.
7. When flowers are dry, remove from paper and store in a covered container for later use.

Fig. 1

Doll Cake

To make a doll cake you will need

Skirt mold; or bundt pan; or 8- and 9-inch layer
pans and a 7- or 8-inch metal or ovenproof
glass bowl
Doll or doll pick
Buttercream Icing
#14, #47, #104 and #101s tubes
Decorating comb

Molds for the skirt can be purchased or the
skirt can be made by using a bundt pan or round
cake pans in conjunction with a small bowl.

How to make the skirt using the mold

1. Bake the cake according to package instructions. Cool and turn out onto a cake plate or
   doily-covered cardboard.
2. Insert the doll or doll pick in the top. If using a
   whole doll, cover the bottom half and hair
   with plastic wrap before inserting.

How to make the skirt using the bundt pan

1. Follow steps 1 and 2 above.
2. Make a cardboard cone to fit the doll's waist,
   tapering it into the top of the cake. (Fig. 1)

How to make a skirt using layer pans and a round bowl

1. Follow step 1 under **How to make the skirt
   from a mold**, above, except layer the 9-inch,
   8-inch and bowl cakes, icing between each
   layer. (Fig. 2)
2. Insert a doll or doll pick in the top center of the
   cake. If using a whole doll, make a small hole
   in the top of the cake. Cover the bottom half of
   the doll and the hair, then insert the doll up to
   the waist.
3. Trim the layers to form a smooth, tapered skirt.

How to decorate a doll cake (Figures, p. 36)

1. Using the #14 tube, cover the bodice with tiny
   stars. A collar or scoop neckline can be incor-
   porated into the bodice design. The arms may
   be left bare; or make short, puffed sleeves.
   (Fig. 1)
2. Ice the top four inches of the skirt quite heavily.
   (Fig. 2)
3. Using a toothpick, mark a panel in front and
   six evenly divided sections around the top of
   the skirt. Mark six corresponding sections at
   the base of the skirt directly under the top
   marks. (Fig. 2)
4. Use the #47 tube or decorating comb to make
   vertical lines in the front panel. (Fig. 3)
5. Starting on one side of the front panel, use a
   decorating comb to make a horizontal scallop
   in each of the top sections. (Fig. 3)
6. Starting at the bottom, use the #104 tube to
   make fluted garlands. Work up row by row, following the scallops in the top section. (See
   FLUTED GARLAND, page 52). (Fig. 4)
7. Use the #14 tube to make tiny stars at the
   base of the skirt where the scallops come together. (Tiny roses may be added at these
   points also.) (Fig. 4)
8. Use the #14 tube to pipe a border where the
   combed section meets the front panel.
9. Use the #101s tube to form a straight band of
   icing around the waist to make a belt. Add a
   bow with long ends by making a figure eight
   and adding uneven tails. (Or, instead of a belt,
   a little peplin can be made around the waist
   with the #104 tube, using the fluted garland
   technique as shown in the photo on page 35.)
   (Fig. 5)

Alternate Methods

Dolls may be decorated by simply covering the
skirt with stars or by icing the skirt and then
texturing the icing with a small spatula as shown
in the background of the photo on page 35.

Doll picks and a whole doll

Fig. 1

Fig. 2

Fig. 1

Fig. 4

Fig. 2

Fig. 5

Fig. 3

Clowns
(See cake on front cover.)

Clowns can be piped onto a cake in various positions: climbing over the cake, standing beside the cake, arms resting on the cake top, lying on their stomachs, and so on. They make delightful decorations for children's cakes.

To make clowns you will need
Buttercream Icing
#7 tube
#102 tube
#2 tube

How to make a clown
1. Body: Use the #7 tube to form an elongated shape, slightly larger at the bottom than at the top. (Fig. 6)
2. Arms and hands: Push the tube into the top of the body on each side and apply pressure to pull out arms and hands. (Fig. 7)
   Note When adding legs or arms to a figure, always insert the tube before applying pressure, so that the arm or leg will appear to be growing from the body.
3. Legs and feet: Push the tube into the bottom of the body and pull out legs and feet. (Fig. 8)
4. Details: Use the #102 tube, in the same or contrasting color, to add ruffles to the wrists, ankles, neck and bottom of shirt.
5. Use the #2 tube to add buttons to the front of the shirt and balls to the tips of the shoes.
6. Head: Push the #7 tube into the neck and form a large ball for the head. Pipe a peaked hat on top with a ball at the end. Add hair and desired features. (Optional: Use a plastic clown head to complete.) (Fig. 9)

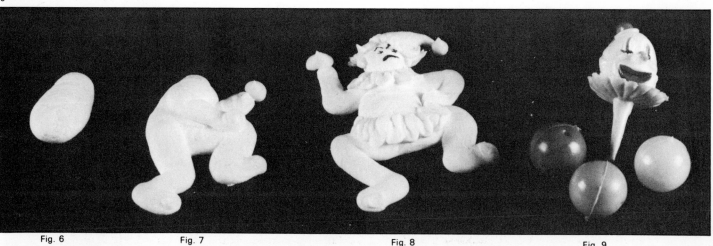

Fig. 6   Fig. 7   Fig. 8   Fig. 9

Lesson 10 More Flowers

Pop-Ups
(See cake on page 42.)

To make pop-ups you will need
#17 or other star tube, white, lavender,
  or pale pink icing
#4 tube, yellow icing

Use these unusual flowers for Canterbury
bells or fill-ins with other flowers. Pop-ups should
be made on a solid surface such as a practice
board or tray.

How to make pop-ups
1. Hold the #17 tube perpendicular to and lightly resting on the surface of the board.
2. Apply very heavy pressure and let the flower
   pop up around the tube. Release pressure and
   remove the tube.(Fig. 1)
   Note Squeeze the bag hard but *do not* push it
   downward. The tube should rest only *lightly*
   on the surface of the board.
3. Use the #4 tube to draw one stamen up from
   the inside of the flower.
4. Pick up flowers with the tip of a paring knife
   and, sliding them off the knife with the end of
   a flower nail, place them on the cake as
   desired.

Carnation
(See cake on page 42.)

To make carnations you will need
Flower Decorator Icing
Waxed paper squares
#7 flower nail
#103 tube

It is important that the icing is stiff, so that the
petals ruffle properly.

How to make carnations
1. Attach a waxed paper square to the nail with
   a dot of icing.

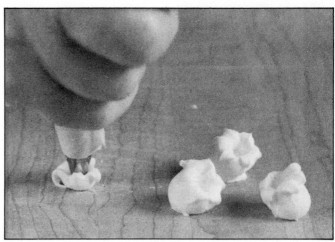

Fig. 1

2. Holding the tube about ½ inch from the center
   of the nail, make a very ruffled petal, using
   short bursts of pressure to make the tiny
   ruffles. (Fig. 2)
   Note It is important that the wrist move rapidly
   to form the petals.
3. Complete a circle of ruffled petals.
4. Starting almost in the center, make a second
   row of petals, angling them up slightly. Make
   these petals shorter than the first row. (Fig. 3)
5. Angle the tube higher and start in the center
   to add a third row of very short and ruffled
   petals. (Fig. 4)
   Note The center of the flower should be a bit
   concave.
6. Fill the center with a circle of tiny stand-up
   petals. (Fig. 5)

Half Carnation
To make a half carnation you will need
Flower Decorator Icing
Waxed paper squares
#7 Flower nail
#103 tube
#4 tube, green Buttercream Icing

Fig. 2-6

Fig. 1-4

How to make a half carnation (Fig. 6, p. 37)

1. Following steps 1 and 2, above, make ruffled petals in a semicircle.
2. Add the second and third rows, making each shorter than the preceding one and coming in a little closer to the center of the flower.
3. Fill the center with a calyx made with a #4 tube.
4. Add a stem and thin, elongated leaves which curl at the ends, still using the #4 tube.

Wild Rose
(See cake on page 55.)

To make wild roses you will need
Flower Decorator Icing
Waxed paper squares
#7 flower nail
#104 tube, pink icing
#1 tube, yellow icing or small yellow stamens

How to make wild roses

1. Attach a waxed paper square to the nail with a dot of icing.
2. Place the wide end of the #104 tube at a 45° angle in the center of the nail. Make a fan petal, tipping the narrow end of the tube up slightly, and turning the nail a little to complete the petal. The right edge of the fan petal should be tipped up just a little so that the next petal can be started just under the edge of it. (Fig. 5)

Fig. 5-7

3. Make five petals, tipping up the right edge of each petal and starting each just under the edge of the preceding one. When the last petal is completed, bring the tube up perpendicular to the nail to avoid touching the first petal. (Fig. 6)
4. Add a small cluster of short yellow stamens in the center of the flower or make a cluster of small yellow dots with the #1 tube. (Fig. 7)

Poinsettia
(See cake on opposite page.)

To make poinsettias you will need
Flower Decorator or Royal Icing
Waxed paper squares
#7 Flower Nail
Parchment bag, bright red icing, cut ∧
Parchment bag, green icing, cut with a small opening
Parchment bag, yellow icing, cut ∧ with a small opening
Red food coloring

How to make poinsettias

1. Attach a waxed paper square to the nail with a dot of icing.
2. Starting about ½ inch from the center of the nail, form elongated leaves in a circle, using the bag with red icing. Make some leaves shorter than others. (Fig. 1)
3. Starting closer to the center of the nail, add a second row of leaves, making them shorter than those of the first row. (Fig. 2)
4. Make a third row of small leaves which come almost to the center. (Fig. 3)
5. Pipe a cluster of small green balls in the center of the red leaves, using the bag with green icing. (Fig. 4)
6. Add tiny yellow balls on top of each of the green balls, using the bag with yellow icing.
7. Use a fine artist's brush to add a small dot of red food color to each yellow ball. (Fig. 4)
8. Remove waxed paper with complete flower from the nail and allow to dry.

Poinsettia Cake Flowers and leaves, cut parchment cones; shell border, #32 tube; scallops on cake top, #2 tube
Wreath Cake Wreath base, #32 tube; leaves, leaf-cut parchment cone; candles, #16 tube; flame and berries, #4 tube; bow, #101 tube; borders, #32 tube

Lesson 11
Run Sugar

Making the Icing

1. Bring two egg whites to room temperature. Measure and add an equal amount of water. Beat with an electric mixer at slow speed until foamy.
2. Add finely sifted confectioners' sugar a small amount at a time; or, for a stronger icing, add commercial Royal Icing mix which has been finely sifted. Beat until smooth after each addition.
3. Test the icing as it thickens by dropping a small amount from the tip of a spoon onto waxed paper. The icing should smooth itself in 4 to 5 seconds. If the icing runs too much, add more sugar.
4. Cover icing with a damp cloth or store in a tightly covered container. Let icing rest at least two hours or, for best results, overnight, to allow air bubbles to escape. Before using the icing, run a knife through it several times to remove any remaining bubbles.

Running in the pattern

Patterns can be chosen from art or coloring books, but whatever is used must have lines distinct enough to be clearly seen through waxed paper.

1. Place the pattern on a flat, sturdy surface which can be moved later. Do not tape the pattern down.
2. Cover the pattern with waxed paper and secure the waxed paper with tape.
3. Select the colors to be used and color the run sugar icing. Color small amounts of Royal Icing the same colors for use in outlining.
4. Outline the pattern using Royal Icing and a #1 or #2 tube. Where two colors come together, outline only one color.
5. Partially fill parchment bags with run sugar as needed for each color. Fold tops down securely. Cut a small opening in the tip of the bag. Flood the outlined areas, working quickly from side to side, so that no area dries so much that it will not flow together. Be sure that the run sugar comes up to the outline, barely covers it, but does not flow beyond it. Mound icing slightly in the center of the area being filled. There should be no low areas which will weaken the finished piece.

Run sugar work can also be done with no outline. The icing must be quite heavy but of a consistency that will smooth itself in 8 to 10 seconds.

1. Run the icing almost to the pattern edge; then, with a fine quality artist's brush, bring the icing to the edge of the section, working quickly.
2. Allow each color of icing to dry somewhat before adding the next color.

Finishing the pieces

1. Allow the piece to dry completely.
2. Cut the tape on one side of the waxed paper and slide the pattern from under the run-in piece.
3. Paint in details with a fine brush and food coloring, using the pattern as a guide. A few features, a little shading, or a bit of detail makes a great difference in a finished piece.

Removing the finished piece

1. Allow the finished piece to dry at least 24 hours. Run sugar dries best in dry, clear weather or at controlled room temperature.
2. Pulling gently on the waxed paper, move the finished piece to the edge of the table. *Do Not* pull the finished piece up from the waxed paper.
3. Hold one hand under the piece and with the other hand, pull the waxed paper from the bottom, working from side to side.

This is a *fragile* piece of icing; handle it with extreme care. If the piece is still soft underneath, carefully turn it over and dry it. To make the finished piece sturdier, run-in the bottom with more icing.

Run sugar can be made in advance and will keep for about one week. To use, rebeat it, then allow it to settle for a few hours. If the icing becomes flat, add more egg whites and confectioners' sugar or Royal Icing mix.

Patterns can be run directly on the cake for last-minute work. They will dry enough in an hour to lightly paint with food coloring, although they will still be soft in the center.

Lesson 12
Royal Icing Flowers

Fig. 1-3

Fig. 4-6

Daisies
(See cake on page 19.)

Following are instructions for making two types of daisies, one with a rounded petal, the other with a more pointed petal. Both may be made directly on the cake, or they can be made in advance using a flower nail. The advantage in making them in advance is that they can be curved as they dry.

To make daisies you will need
Royal Icing
Waxed paper squares
#7 Flower nail
#104 tube
#233 tube, egg yellow icing

How to make daisies using the #101 tube
1. Attach a waxed paper square to the flower nail with a dot of icing. Place a tiny dot of icing in the center of the waxed paper to be used as a guide when forming the flowers.
2. Hold the tube at a 45° angle in the center of the nail. Apply moderate pressure and slide the tube toward the outside of the nail, swiveling the tube as the petal reaches the outside edge of the nail. Bring the tube back sharply to the center, releasing pressure as it reaches the center. Keep the center flat and the petals narrow for a natural look. (Fig. 1 and 2)

3. To form the center, hold the #233 tube perpendicular to the center of the nail. Apply pressure and, after the center is formed, release with a sharp upward motion. (Fig. 3)
4. Slide the waxed paper with the daisy off the nail and dry flat or on a curved plastic former (Available in three sizes at cake decorating supply outlets).
   Note Daisies can also be curved as they dry by placing them on the cardboard tubes from waxed paper or paper toweling. They can be partially curved by propping them on one edge of a jelly roll pan.

How to make daisies using the #104 tube
1. Attach a waxed paper square to the nail with a dot of icing. Put a tiny dot of icing in the center of the square to be used as a guide when placing the petals.
2. Hold the #104 tube perpendicular to the nail, the wide end at the outside edge and slightly above the nail. Apply a small amount of pressure, bringing the petal from the outside toward the dot in the center. Fill the nail with petals, bringing each one toward the dot of icing. (Fig. 4 and 5)
3. Complete the daisy by following Step 3 above, using the #233 tube.
4. Dry as described above.

Clockwise from the top
Carnation Cake Carnations, #103 tube; wild roses, #104 tube; top border (modified reverse scroll); base border, #32 tube; side scroll, #4 tube; writing and top border trim, cut parchment cone
Heart Cake Pop-ups, #16 tube; stem, #4 tube; leaves, leaf-cut parchment cone; writing, #1 tube; top border, #16 tube; bottom border, #32 tube; border trim and piped hearts, #4 tube
Rosebud Sheet Cake Borders, #14 tube; laydown rose, #104 tube

Fig. 1-4

Zinnias
(See cake on page 62.)

To make zinnias you will need
Royal Icing
Waxed paper squares
#7 Flower nail
#101 tube
#1 or #233 tube

How to make zinnias
1. Hold the #101 tube at a 45° angle with the wide end toward the center of the nail, leaving a ⅜-inch opening in the center. Apply pressure and make a row of tiny, slightly elongated petals. (Fig. 1)
2. Make a second row of tiny petals, not quite as long as the first row and filling in toward the center somewhat. (Fig. 2)
3. Make a third row of petals, again closer to the center than the second row. There should be a slightly concave center in the flower. (Fig. 3)
4. Fill the center with tiny yellow or green dots using either the #1 or #233 tube. (Fig. 4)

Miniature Roses
To make miniature roses you will need
#101s tube, Pink Royal or Flower Decorator Icing
½-inch waxed paper squares
Round toothpick (to be used as a flower nail)

How to make miniature roses
1. Slide a square of waxed paper halfway down the toothpick.
2. Using the #101s tube, touch the toothpick with the icing and wrap a center around the upper portion of the toothpick. (Fig. 5)
3. Add two or three small petals close to the center. (Fig. 6)

4. Add four or five petals around the three petals, making them more opened. (See ROSES, page 16 for more detail on how to form petals.) Turn the toothpick as you would a flower nail when forming the petals. (Fig. 7)
5. Slide the waxed paper up under the flower and push the flower off the toothpick.
6. If desired, add five green sepals to the back of each rose to make it more realistic.

Use the small rose centers as tiny rosebuds; the center with two or three petals as a half-opened rose; the completed rose as a full-blown rose.

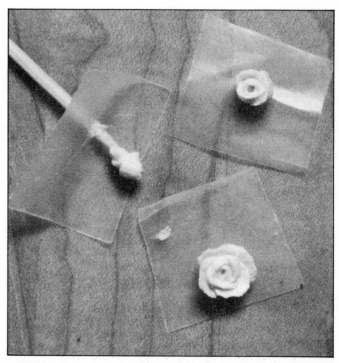

Fig. 5-7

Lesson 13
More Royal Icing Flowers

Violets
(See cake on page 55.)

To make violets you will need
Royal Icing
½-inch waxed paper squares
#7 Flower nail
#101 or #101s tube, purple icing
#1 tube, yellow icing

How to make violets (Fig. 1)
1. Attach a waxed paper square to the nail with a dot of icing.
2. Using the #101 or #101s tube, make three fan petals, covering half of the nail, overlapping them slightly.
3. Add two elongated petals on the remaining half of the nail, separating them from the fan petals.
4. Add two tiny yellow teardrops to the center using the #1 tube.

Apple Blossoms
To make apple blossoms you will need
Royal Icing
#1 flower nail
#101 or #101s tube, pink icing
#1 tube, yellow icing

How to make apple blossoms
1. Attach a waxed paper square to the nail with a dot of icing.
2. Place the wide end of the tube at a 45° angle in the center of the nail. Make a fan petal, tipping the narrow end of the tube up slightly, and turning the nail a little to complete the petal. The right edge of the fan petal should be tipped up just a little so that the next petal can be started just under the edge of it. (Fig. 2)
3. Make five rounded petals, tipping up the right edge of each petal and starting each just under the edge of the preceding one. When the last petal is completed, bring the tube up perpendicular to the nail to avoid touching the first petal. (Fig. 3-4)
4. Use the #1 tube to make several very tiny yellow dots in the center.

Fig. 1

Fig. 2-4

Fig. 1-3

Petunias

(See cake on opposite page)

To make petunias you will need
Royal Icing
4-inch lightweight foil squares
#12 Lily nail
Vegetable shortening
#104 tube, white, purple, pink or red icing
#16 tube, light green icing
Yellow stamens

How to make petunias
1. Fit a square of foil into the flower nail and tuck it around the rim. Lightly coat the foil with shortening.
2. Place the wide end of the #104 tube down into the nail. Apply pressure to make an inverted cone. (Fig. 1)
3. Starting at the top edge of the cone of icing make six very ruffled petals. Begin each petal against the top of the cone. Using heavy pressure with a slight jiggling motion, move the tube upward, swivel it up over the rim and back down. Keep the tube quite flat. Avoid an opening where the petals meet and in the center of the petal. (Fig. 2)
4. Using the #16 tube, pipe a small star into the throat of the flower. (Fig. 3)
5. If desired, add a small cluster of short yellow stamens in the green star.
6. Carefully remove the foil and flower from the nail and let the flower dry.
7. Ease the foil carefully from the nail and allow the flower to dry. When dry, carefully remove the foil. If the foil is difficult to remove, warm the flower very slightly in a 100° oven; then gently work the foil from the flower.

Poppy

(See cake on page 14.)

To make poppies you will need
Poppy Red Royal or Flower Decorator Icing
Waxed paper squares
#7 flower nail
#104 tube
Black stamens

How to make poppies
1. Attach a waxed paper square to the nail with a dot of icing.
2. Place the wide end of the tube in the center of the nail. Apply a great deal of pressure and swivel the tube, jiggling it slightly, moving the wide end toward the outside of the nail and then back to the center. End with the wide end of the tube at the beginning point in the center of the nail. (Fig. 4)

Fig. 4-5

Top
Petunia Cake Petunias, #103 tube; top border, #69 tube (ruffles) and #4 tube; bottom border, #32 and #4 tubes; writing and bottom border trim, cut parchment cone
Bottom
Jonquil Cake Jonquils, #104, #4 tubes and cut parchment cone; borders, #16 tube

3. Make three more of the above petal, turning the nail after each one, overlapping each petal slightly. (Fig. 5)
4. Hold the tube nearly upright, wide end down, in the center of the petals. Applying very little pressure, swivel the tube to form a small upright petal. Make two more petals following this procedure. (Fig. 5)
5. Paint the center of the poppy as shown with black paste food color.
6. Insert a few black stamens in the center of the flower.

Easter Lily
(See cake on page 51.)
To make Easter lilies you will need
Royal Icing
4-inch lightweight foil squares
#12 Lily nail
Vegetable shortening
#352 tube, white icing
6 Yellow stamens

How to make Easter lilies
1. Fit a square of foil into the flower nail and tuck it around the rim. Coat the foil lightly with shortening.

2. Use the #352 tube to make six petals. (For a thinner, more fragile petal, use a parchment bag cut ∧.) Start at the bottom inside the nail and apply moderate pressure; move upwards, gradually decreasing pressure and pulling the petal to a point just over the rim of the nail as pressure is released. (Fig. 1) Make six petals spaced per instructions for JONQUILS on page 27. Avoid filling the center of the lily. The petals should barely come together at the bottom, overlapping only slightly.
Note If the petal breaks off and does not pull out to a point, the icing is probably too thick. Remove it from the bag and soften with a little water before starting over.
3. Place stamens in the center of the flower, trimming them so that they are only slightly higher than the rim of the flower. (Fig. 2)
4. Carefully ease the foil from the nail and allow the flower to dry. (See PETUNIAS, page 47, for tips on how to remove foil.)

Make more lilies than needed, since the petals are fragile and may break when the flower is removed from the foil.

Fig. 1-2

Dried Easter Lily

Lesson 14
Sugar and Chocolate Molding

Sugar Molding
Sugar molding is done using commercial molds into which a sugar-water mixture is pressed and then allowed to dry.

Sugar Mixture
Mix 2 cups of granulated sugar and 4 teaspoons water by hand until thoroughly blended.
Note To color the sugar before it is molded, blend food coloring with the water before adding it to the sugar, so that the color will mix evenly with the sugar.

Test the sugar for moldability by squeezing a little in your hand. When your hand is opened, the sugar should retain an exact handprint. If the sugar crumbles, add a few drops of water and blend well.

How to mold sugar
1. Firmly press moistened sugar into a clean, dry mold. Level the top of the sugar with a knife or spatula; remove any excess.
2. Place a piece of cardboard over the mold and invert the molded sugar onto the cardboard.
3. Remove the mold immediately. Dry the sugar for several hours before using.
4. Decorate, if desired, by painting with thinned Royal Icing or colored piping gel.

Hollow Sugar Bells
To make sugar bells you will need
Bell mold
Small artificial flowers
Colored edible glitter

How to make bells
1. Allow sugar mold to dry for thirty minutes, or until the outside of the bell is dry and hard.
2. Place the bell in your left hand and carefully scoop out the soft sugar with a small plastic knife, spoon, or similar tool.
3. Pipe a small ball of Royal Icing inside at the top and secure tiny flowers in the icing.
4. Pipe a thin line of Royal Icing around the rim of the bell and immediately dip the iced rim into the glitter.

Chocolate Molding
Plastic molds are available in hundreds of patterns and can be used for both sugar and chocolate molding. They are available at cake decorating supply outlets. Use molds in combination with other decorating techniques to create delightful cakes such as those on pages 26 and 30 (Cameo and Cowboys and Indians).

To mold chocolate you will need
Mold
Chocolate-flavored coating(s), brown or colored (available at most cake decorating supply outlets)

How to mold chocolate
Note Molds must be clean and dry before using.
1. If desired, use a soft artist's brush to paint the inside of the mold with colored coating. Melt coating over hot, not boiling, water. Paint the inside according to the mold pattern or as desired. Chill in freezer after each color is added to prevent colors from running together.
2. Use either brown or colored coating and fill the mold. To do so, melt chocolate coating as above. Pour into mold. Chill in the freezer until the mold appears cloudy, showing the chocolate has shrunk from it.
3. Turn the mold and the piece will drop out easily.

Lesson 15
More Borders

Shell-Up, Bottom of Cake Border (Fig. 1)
(See cake on opposite page)
To make a shell-up border you will need
Boiled or Buttercream Icing
#4 tube
#32 tube

How to make a shell-up border
1. Hold the tube perpendicular to the cake plate and pointed down, just above the cake plate and slightly away from the cake.
2. Apply pressure, keeping the tube under the surface of the icing, and move the tube a little toward you and then up and against the cake, forming a tail as pressure is released. As the shell builds out, it will also build down to the cake plate, forming a fan which tapers to an end up on the cake.
3. Circle the cake with shells.
4. Start above the tails, about two inches above the cake plate, and drop three strings which overlap the shells. The longest string should come to one-quarter inch above the cake board, the other two strings should be consecutively shorter. The first set of strings starts at shell 1 and attaches to shell 3. The second set of strings starts at shell 2 and attaches to shell 4, etc.

5. If desired, finish with tiny balls of icing placed at the points where the strings come together.

Shell-Down, Top of Cake Border (Fig. 2)
(See cake on page 26.)
To make a shell-down border you will need
Boiled or Buttercream Icing
#32 tube
#2 tube

How to make a shell-down border
1. Hold the tube perpendicular to the cake plate, pointing it up just below the top edge of the cake and slightly away from it.
2. Apply pressure and build the shell up slightly over the top of the cake, keeping the tube under the surface of the icing and moving the tube slightly toward you and then down to the cake. The shell should be fanned out at the top and tapered at the bottom.
3. Continue making shells around the top of the cake, placing them so that they almost touch.
4. Use the #2 tube to add double overlapped drop work at the tail of each shell, starting each string the same distance from the top of the cake. This will camouflage any uneven tails.
5. Drop two short strings, one slightly longer than the other, from the fullest point of each shell, reaching to the next shell.

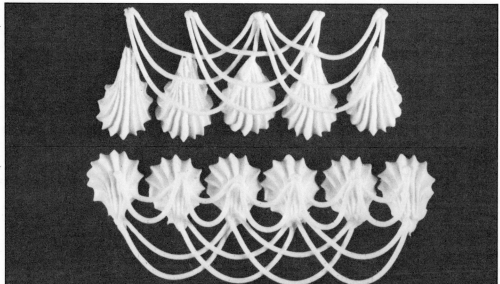

Fig. 1/Shell-Up Border

Fig. 2/Shell-Down Border

Church Window and Lily Church window, piping gel in small parchment cones; lilies, cut parchment cone and artificial stamens; leaves, leaf-cut parchment cone; top border, #16 tube; bottom border, #32 and #4 tubes

Overlay Shell (Fig. 1)

To make an overlay shell border you will need
Boiled or Buttercream Icing
#32 tube
#4 tube

How to make an overlay shell border
1. Use the #32 tube to make a border of large shells around the top edge of the cake. (See SHELL BORDER, page 13.)
2. Using the #4 tube, make a tiny circular motion to form a lay-down question mark on the side of each shell.
3. Use the #4 tube to overlay a straight line on each question mark. The tail of each question mark should be tucked behind the next shell.

Bulb and Drop (Fig. 2)
(See cake on page 58.)

To make a bulb and drop border you will need
Boiled or Buttercream Icing
#4 tube

This is a side border used on top of the tier. It is important to have the cake neatly iced with a smooth area where the top and side come together.

How to make a bulb and drop border.
1. Make a round ball using bulb work technique at the top of the cake side, keeping the tube under the surface of the icing. Without releasing pressure, pull a string straight out about 1¼ to 1½ inches from the ball.
2. Bring the string across and attach it to the top of the cake as desired.
3. Midway between the ball and the end of the string make another ball. Pull out a string the same length as the first and attach it just beyond the ball.
4. The third ball, and each succeeding ball, will be formed over the end of the attached string. When the border has completely surrounded the cake, tuck the end of the last string under the first string. It cannot be attached at the top of the cake as the others, but can be tucked slightly under the beginning string and will appear similar to the others.

The most important things to remember when making this border are: (1.) Make the ball full and round, and (2.) draw the string straight out from the ball and swing it across to attach.

Ruffled or Fluted Borders (Fig. 3 and 4)
(See cakes on pages 35 and 58.)

To make a fluted or ruffled border you will need
Boiled or Buttercream Icing
#104 tube

This side border can be used as a ruffled skirt on a Doll Cake (see page 35) or can be draped to form a garland.

How to make a ruffled or fluted garland
1. Hold the wide end of the #104 tube up. Tip the narrow end of the tube toward the left, almost parallel to the cake, but with the fine edge tipped out slightly. Move the tube up and down slightly to form the ruffled border, gradually arching the tube down to the bottom center and tipping the narrow end to the right at the right side as the garland is completed. The tube should remain almost parallel to the cake with the narrow end pointing out as it tips down and then to the right. The wrist should swivel to achieve the correct motion.
2. To form a fluted garland, hold the tube as described above, but form each small section deliberately. For each section, use a slight downward motion, applying a burst of pressure at the bottom point to help form the drape, then releasing pressure as the tube comes up a bit less and forms the curved garland.

Both of these garlands can be made double by starting the second slightly above the first one and tipping the bottom of the tube out enough to clear the lower garland. (Fig. 5)

Drop work adds a beautiful finishing touch to this border.

Use the ruffled or fluted border on the lower tier of a cake since it is heavier than other borders.

Fig. 1/Overlay Shell

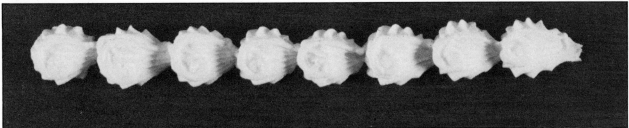

Fig. 2/Bulb and Drop

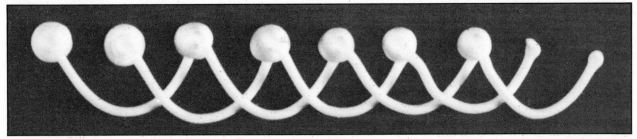

Fig. 3/Ruffled Garland

Fig. 4/Fluted Garland

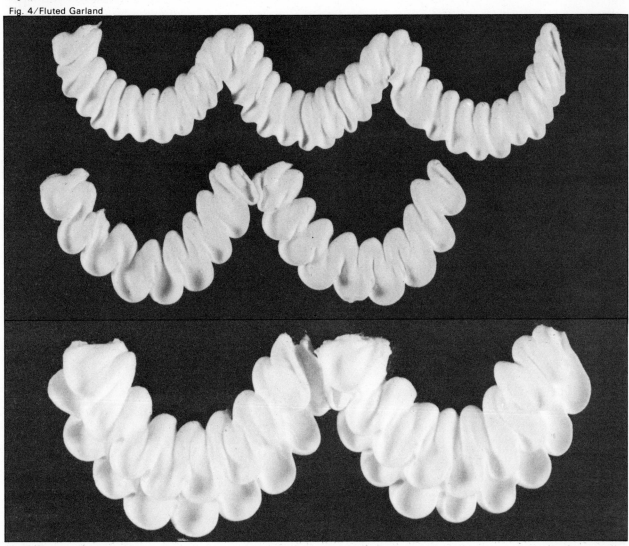

Fig. 5/Double Fluted Garland

Scroll Side Border
(See cake on page 55)

To make a scroll side border you will need
Boiled or Buttercream Icing
#4 tube

How to make a scroll side border
1. Using Fig. 1 as a guide, mark the pattern of the border in the icing with a toothpick. With practice, you will be able to do it freehand.
2. Form a series of lay-down question marks, each one beginning in the tail of the last one. The basic pattern is then overpiped using a circular motion, tapering into the end of the question mark where the next question mark fits into it.
3. Add small curved lines as shown to complete the design.

Reverse Scroll Side Border
To make the reverse scroll border you will need
Boiled or Buttercream Icing
#4 tube

How to make a reverse scroll border (Fig. 2)
1. Make a smooth curved line around the entire cake.
2. Using a circular motion, pipe a graceful C into each curve of the line, graduating the size of the C until it tapers into the base line just before reaching the next C.
   Note Every other C will be upside down, but all will face the same direction.
3. Add smaller C's to the center of each curve, using a smooth line, again tapering the end into the base line.

Fig. 1/Scroll Side Border

Fig. 2/Reverse Scroll Side Border

Top
Wild Rose, Sweet Pea and Violet Cake Wild rose, #104 tube; sweet peas and violets, #101 tube; bottom shell border, #32 tube; side drop border, #2 tube; leaves, leaf-cut parchment cone; top trim, #101 tube
Bottom
Pansy Cake Pansies, #104 tube; bottom shell, #32 tube; side reverse scroll, #4 tube; writing, leaves and top scallop, cut parchment cone; top border, #4 tube; side drop border, #4 tube

Lesson 16
Wedding Cakes

Next to birthday cakes, wedding cakes are certainly the most popular special occasion cake; and cake decorators are often called upon to design the wedding cake of a family member or friend. Because traditional wedding cakes are tiered and ornately designed, this lesson is devoted to teaching the fundamentals of wedding cake design.

Choice of Cake

For ease of handling, decorating and transporting, always use a firm cake. Bake the cake several days prior to the wedding day to allow sufficient time to decorate it. The cake *must* be crumb frosted with Buttercream Icing immediately after cooling and then rather heavily iced as soon as the crumb coat of icing has dried. This seals the cake and keeps it moist.

Tier Sizes

A balanced cake should have a minimum three inch difference in tier size, such as 6-9-12 inches or 7-11-15 inches. Tiers should also be either the same height or each layer should be uniformly shorter than the one below it. A cake having a three-inch high bottom tier and a four-inch high top tier will look unbalanced.

Baking the Cake

Large or thick layers which require long baking times should be protected from baking too rapidly or over browning. To prevent overbrowning, cut strips of sheeting or toweling and fold several times to the depth of the cake pan. Wet the cloth thoroughly and pin it securely around the outside of the pan. With the wet cloth, the outside will not brown and the cake will bake flat. (Reusable "Magi Cake Strips" are commercially available at cake decorating supply outlets.)

Cool cake in pans or racks for ten to twenty minutes before turning out. After turning cake out of pans onto a rack, immediately place another rack over the bottom of the cake and turn right side up to finish cooling.

Preparing the Cake for Decorating

Remove brown tops from the cakes, so that when the cake is cut, no brown will appear through the center. Trim to level, if necessary, using a serrated knife. Place the bottom layer, trimmed side up, on a prepared board or separator plate. Small layers are easy to position, but large layers require care.

To place a fourteen- to twenty-inch layer topside down on the bottom layer, follow these instructions:

1. Ice the bottom layer and allow it to dry until a light crust forms.
2. Place a large baking sheet (without sides) or a large tray on the layer to be positioned.
3. Place one hand under the center of the rack on which the cake is resting. Place the other hand on the center of the baking sheet which is resting on the cake.
4. Lift the cake and both trays or racks off the table and carefully and quickly flip them so that the cake now rests, topside down, on the baking sheet.
5. Holding the tray on each side, gently shake the tray to slide the cake into position on the bottom layer.
   Note If the icing on the bottom layer is still very soft, the top layer must be carefully positioned. It cannot be moved once it is placed on the icing.
6. Crumb frost the tier immediately. (See page 6.) Thin the icing with a little water to make the crumb icing easier to spread. Allow the icing to dry.
7. Spread a generous layer of Buttercream Icing on the cake layer.

Corners of square cakes often bake lower than the rest of the cake. To level corners, tuck pieces of cake trimmings between the layers at the corners. Seal with a small amount of icing.

Icing

For the whitest Buttercream Icing, use water

and clear vanilla. Buttercream made with milk and brown vanilla will be ivory color.

Boiled Icing is excellent for border and string work, but it should not be used on the entire wedding cake, since it will not keep the cake moist. It is best used for border work on cakes iced with Buttercream Icing.

Decorating the Cake

How simple or elaborate a wedding cake is to be decorated depends on the bride's choice as well as the experience of the decorator. There are no rules telling a decorator how to design a wedding cake, but we do offer a few suggestions which can serve as guidelines.

1. When in doubt, simplify. A simply decorated cake is more elegant than an overly decorated cake.
2. No decoration at all is more attractive than a sloppily decorated cake. Neatness and precision are both extremely important to the artistic execution of a wedding cake.
3. Do not use unfamiliar designs on a wedding cake. Practice new, difficult or complicated borders on small family cakes or a practice board until you are comfortable with them before attempting the design on a wedding cake.
4. When using an elaborate floral design, simplify the border work. Conversely, if using only a few flowers, the border work can be very elaborate.
5. When using side borders, use the heaviest on the bottom tier and then design each successively higher tier with a lighter weight border.
6. To evenly space garlands, mark the icing using your own pattern or a commercial garland marker. To mark the icing, cut waxed paper the same size as the tier and fold into the number of sections needed. Place over the cake tier and mark sections in the icing with a toothpick.

Cake Stands

Grecian Pillar Stands

The most widely used cake separators are the Wilton and Bush Grecian pillar stands. Each has two plates, four pillars, and four pegs which go through the bottom tier of the cake. Select a size with tier plates which will be at least one-half inch larger than each iced cake tier so that there is room for border work. Select a plate or use a covered board four inches larger than the bottom tier.

Assemble the cake as follows:

1. Place the bottom tier on the plate or covered board. (A practical and attractive cake board can be constructed with ⅝-inch to ⅞-inch plywood, 4 inches larger than the diameter of the cake and covered with white adhesive-backed paper or colored foil, which is available in many colors.)
2. Place cakes on their respective plates.
3. Insert pegs into plate.
4. Repeat Steps 2-3 for each tier.
5. Decorate tiers.
6. Assemble cake by securing pillars.

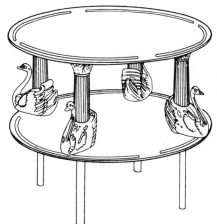

Bush Grecian Pillar Stand

Wilton Grecian Pillar Stand

"Super Strong" Cake Stand

Country Kitchen has a unique set of separators called "Super Strong" which has several advantages over other separators. With the "Super Strong," each cake layer sits on a translucent plate. This base plate rests on a white plate to which long pointed legs are attached. These legs are inserted through the cake, which rests on the upper translucent plate, and serve both as pillars and pegs.

This translucent plate is one inch high and is iced as is the cake, making the tiers appear taller. In selecting the separators, choose plates which are the same size as the cake tiers.

Assemble the cake as follows:

1. Place tiers on their respective translucent plates and decorate.
2. Insert the legs with attached plate through the top of the next tier.
3. Transport the tiers separately.
4. To assemble, place each translucent plate on its supporting white plate and revolve to align the pillars with those on the bottom tier. Position the best side of the cake in front.

Lace Cake Stands

The "Lace Cake Stand" by the Wilton Company has a single column which is inserted through the center of each tier. The column is made of unassembled sections so the cake can be delivered unassembled. The bottom of each plate is slightly concave.

To aid in transportating the cake, follow these steps:

1. Select an empty cake pan for each tier which is slightly smaller than the cake plate. Lay a terrycloth dish towel across each cake pan. Set aside.
2. Place each tier on its cake stand plate; set cake plate in its corresponding pan. The towel keeps the cake plate from sliding.
3. Find the center of each tier, except the top tier, by cutting a sheet of waxed paper into a circle the same size as each cake tier. Fold each circle into eighths. Unfold each and mark the center.
4. Place each circle on top of its corresponding cake tier and mark the center with a toothpick.
5. Remove the waxed paper and cut out the center with the coring tool that is provided.
6. Repeat steps 3-5 for each tier.
7. Decorate the top and sides of each tier.
8. Transport cakes resting on cake pans and assemble at place of reception.

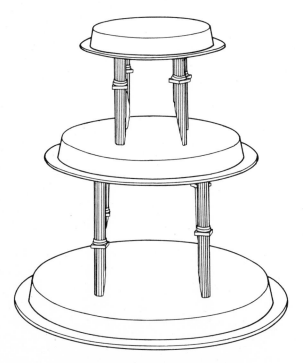

Country Kitchen "Super Strong"

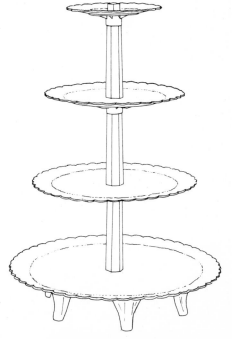

Wilton Lace Cake Stand

Wedding Cake Roses,#104 tube; wild rose, #104 tube; jonquils, #104 and #4 tubes and cut parchment cone; daisies, #104 and #233 tubes; leaves, leaf-cut parchment cone; borders, #4, #32, #16, #104, and #14 tubes

Flat Plates

A stacked cake that will be moved must have supports between the tiers so that it will not sag or lean. Flat plates are available from the Bush Company ranging in even sizes from 6 to 14 inches that have pegs which fit into the bottom.

The pegs are 3½ or 4½ inches long and it is essential that they be the same height as the cake tier. If they are too long, the weight of the tier may cause the legs to move as the cake is transported.

Plastic legs with screws give better support than pegs. Small holes are bored into the flat plates and the legs are firmly attached with flat-headed screws.

To transport a stacked cake follow these steps:
1. Ice the tiers and allow them to dry before stacking. (To prevent the icing from sticking to the supporting plate, sprinkle a small amount of coconut on each tier before stacking.)
2. Stack tiers and decorate.

Crystal Leg Stands

The Wilton Crystal Leg Stand has 7-inch translucent plastic twist legs that go through the cake and serve as both pillar and peg.

How to transport the cake
1. Place the bottom layer on a covered board or plate.
2. Obtain a box for each tier. The box should be at least 7½ inches tall. Lock the top flaps together.
3. Turn the box upside down and cut four holes in the bottom to fit the legs of the cake plate.
4. Attach the legs to the upper plate. If the legs do not fit snugly into the plate, insert a small square of paper napkin into the opening and then secure the legs in place.
5. Set the legs into the holes.
6. Decorate the cake.
7. Lightly mark the icing on each tier where the legs are to go through the cake.
8. At the reception location, lift the cakes from their boxes and assemble them.

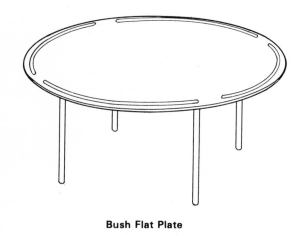

Bush Flat Plate

Wilton Crystal Leg Stand

Cake Mix or Average Size Recipe
Needed for Each Layer

Round

Size	Amount Mix or Recipe
8 inch	2 high layers per box or recipe
9 inch	2 average layers per box or recipe
10 inch	¾ box or recipe
12 inch	1 box or recipe
14 inch	2 boxes or recipes
16 inch	3 boxes or recipes
18 inch	4 boxes or recipes

Square

Size	Amount Mix or Recipe
8 inch	2 average layers per box or recipe
10 inch	1¼ box or recipe
12 inch	2 boxes or recipes
14 inch	3 boxes or recipes
16 inch	4 boxes or recipes

Wedding Cakes—Serving Per Tier

Round Cake

Size	No. Servings
6 inch	12
8 inch	16
9 inch	24
10 inch	36
12 inch	46
13 inch	65
14 inch	76
16 inch	92
17 inch	115
20 inch	140

Square Cake

Size	No. Servings
7 inch	16
10 inch	55
12 inch	85
14 inch	100
16 inch	120
18 inch	140
9 x 13 inch	20
12 x 18 inch	36

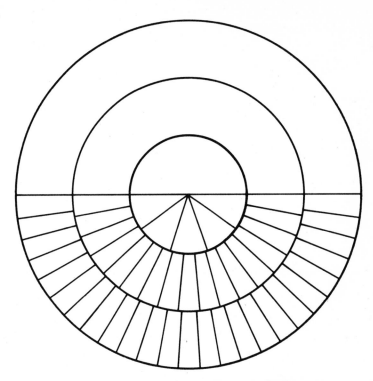

How to Cut a Tiered Cake

The diagram above shows how to cut large cakes by cutting inner circles and then sectioning each into pieces.

Wedding Cakes and Frostings

White Pound Cake

2¾ cups cake flour
1 teaspoon baking soda
1 teaspoon cream of tartar
2½ cups granulated sugar
1 cup plus 3 tablespoons cake flour
1½ cups vegetable shortening or
  high ratio shortening
1 teaspoon salt
1¾ cups egg whites
½ cup milk
¼ teaspoon butter flavoring
1 teaspoon vanilla
½ teaspoon almond flavoring

Sift together the 2¾ cups cake flour, soda and cream of tartar. Set aside. Combine sugar, the remaining cake flour, shortening and salt. Beat for 10 minutes. Alternately mix in dry ingredients and egg whites, beating well after each addition. Slowly add the milk and flavorings. Bake in two greased 9-inch cake pans at 350° for 30 minutes or until cake tests done.

Whipped Chocolate Frosting

A frosting with excellent spreading consistency, it can also be used for borders as well as flowers.

2 cups chopped semisweet chocolate, melted
3 tablespoons flour
1 cup milk
1 cup butter or margarine, softened
1 cup granulated sugar
1½ teaspoons vanilla

Combine melted chocolate and flour in a medium-size saucepan. Blend in milk, a small amount at a time. Cook over medium heat, stirring constantly, until mixture is very thick. Remove from heat and cool completely. In a large mixing bowl, cream butter, sugar and vanilla, beating until light and fluffy. Gradually add cooled chocolate mixture. Beat at high speed until the consistency of whipped cream.

White Chocolate Cake

    1 cup butter, softened
    2 cups granulated sugar
    ¼ pound white chocolate, melted and cooled
    4 eggs
2½ cups cake flour
    ¼ teaspoon baking powder
    ¼ teaspoon salt
    1 cup buttermilk
    1 teaspoon vanilla
    1 cup chopped pecans
    1 cup flaked coconut

Cream butter and sugar until light and fluffy. Add chocolate and blend well. Add eggs, one at a time, beating well after each addition. Sift together dry ingredients. Alternately add dry ingredients and buttermilk, beating well after each addition. Fold in vanilla, pecans and coconut. Pour into 2 greased and floured 9-inch round cake pans. Bake at 350° for 25 minutes, or until a toothpick inserted in the center comes out clean. Cool and frost with White Chocolate Frosting.

White Chocolate Frosting

    ¾ cup white chocolate, melted over low heat
    3 tablespoons flour
    1 cup milk
    1 cup granulated sugar
    1 cup butter
1½ teaspoons vanilla

Stir flour into melted chocolate. Add milk, a little at a time and blend well. Cook over medium heat, stirring constantly, until very thick. Cool completely. In a large mixing bowl, beat sugar, butter and vanilla until light and fluffy. Gradually add cooled chocolate mixture and beat until icing is the consistency of whipped cream.

Fudge Cake

    ⅔ cup butter or margarine, softened
1¾ cups granulated sugar
    2 eggs
    1 teaspoon vanilla
2½ ounces unsweetened baking chocolate, melted
2½ cups sifted cake flour
1¼ teaspoons baking soda
    ½ teaspoon salt
1¼ cups ice water

Prepare two 9-inch layer cake pans by brushing with pan grease*, or grease with shortening, and dust with flour. Cream together the butter, sugar, eggs, vanilla and melted chocolate. Beat until light and fluffy. Sift together the dry ingredients. Alternately mix in dry ingredients with water. Bake at 350° for 30 to 35 minutes or until cake tests done.

*Available at cake decorating supply outlets.

Apple Spice Cake

1½ cups vegetable oil
    2 cups granulated sugar
    4 eggs
    2 cups all-purpose flour
    2 teaspoons baking powder
    1 teaspoon baking soda
    1 teaspoon salt
    2 teaspoons cinnamon
    ½ teaspoon nutmeg
    ¼ teaspoon cloves
    1 teaspoon vanilla
    2 cups grated apple
    1 cup raisins
    1 cup chopped nuts

Blend oil and sugar in a large bowl. Add eggs, one at at time, beating well after each addition. Sift together dry ingredients. Add to oil mixture, beating until smooth. Stir in vanilla, apple, raisins and nuts. Bake in two greased 9-inch round cake pans at 350° for 50 minutes. Frost with Caramel Icing.

Caramel Icing

    ½ cup butter or margarine
    1 cup firmly packed brown sugar
    ¼ teaspoon salt
    6 tablespoons milk
    3 cups confectioners' sugar, sifted

Melt butter in a medium-size saucepan. Stir in brown sugar and salt. Bring to a boil and continue boiling for 2 minutes, stirring constantly and vigorously. Remove from heat and add milk. Return to heat and bring to a rolling boil. Cool to lukewarm. Stir in confectioners' sugar and beat until smooth. Add more milk if necessary.

Zinnia Cake Zinnias, #101 and #1 tube; bottom border, #32 tube; top side border, #4 tube; top trim, #16 and #4 tubes; leaves, leaf-cut parchment cone; lettering, fine artist's brush and food coloring

Index

Cover Photo
Rose Cake Roses #104 tube; stems, writing, drop work, sepals, #4 tube; leaves, ferns, leaf-cut parchment bag; top border, #16 tube, bottom border, #32 tube
Basket Cake Basket weaving, #47 tube, top and bottom borders, #16 tube; instructions for petunias, daisies, zinnias, roses, jonquils, violets, drop flowers, see Index
Clown Cake Clowns #7, #103, #4 tubes and plastic heads; borders and balloon, #4 tube; plastic balloons and wood blocks
Wedding Cake Mums #80 tube; bottom borders, #32 tube, leaves, leaf-cut parchment bag; bottom side garland, #104 and #16 tubes; drop work borders, scroll border, #4 tube; top border, bottom tier, #16 tube